How to Analyze People

The Guide to Read Anyone Like a Magician in 5 Minutes, Analyze and Influece Anyone by Reading Body Language and Speed Read People, Using Human Psychology. Overcome Social Anxiety and Handle Small Talk Easily.

By Jocko Babin & Ray Manson

Table of Contents

liable for any hardship or damages that may befall them after undertaking information described herein.

Additionally, the information in the following pages is intended only for informational purposes and should thus be thought of as universal. As befitting its nature, it is presented without assurance regarding its prolonged validity or interim quality. Trademarks that are mentioned are done without written consent and can in no way be considered an endorsement from the trademark holder.

Introduction

Congratulations on purchasing this book and thank you for doing so.

The human body language is a remarkable thing. It can speak louder than words ever could and deliver messages so impactful when we are at a loss for words. Our bodies give out cues when we love someone, when we hate them, feel angry, when we are sad, happy, and more. It reveals all our innermost thoughts, feelings, desires, moods, and personalities. Whether we realize it or not, our bodies are constantly giving the people around us a glimpse of what may be happening on the inside.

Each day, our body gives out signals throughout the day which reflect the moods we're currently experiencing. It also reflects the situation that we find ourselves in. Without saying a word, our bodies allow others to read and - for the perceptive ones - form a hypothesis about what we may be experiencing or feeling right at that moment. This is called analyzing others, and this is why you've found yourself picking up this book. Because you *want* to better understand the people around you, to get a deeper glimpse into what might be going on.

Over the years, there has been a growing appreciation for the importance of learning how to analyze others. Each chapter of this book is going to address the eight key elements that you must understand in order to *better your understanding* of others. One gesture doesn't just reveal one type of message. Given the context and circumstance, that same gesture could hold several other meanings, and that is what makes body language and learning how to analyze others such an intriguing subject.

There are plenty of books on this subject on the market. Thanks again for choosing this one! Every effort was made to ensure it is full of as much useful information as possible. Please enjoy!

Chapter 1: Knowing Me, Knowing You

It is an intriguing prospect, isn't it? The idea that you could precisely decipher how and what someone is saying without them having to utter a word? The second body language that they are giving off which others might miss. But not you. Because you're perceptive, and you know exactly what to look for when you begin analyzing someone.

When was the last time you stopped to analyze yourself, though?

Before you can begin analyzing someone else, you need to learn how to analyze yourself first. Self-awareness is one of the core principles and a sign that someone possesses emotional intelligence. This key trait is what helps you understand who you are as a person. What your beliefs and your values are as well as the way that you react and respond to others.

When you look at yourself in the mirror, how well do you know the person who is looking back at you? Learning to analyze people is an important skill to have because it can help you strengthen the relationships that you have with them. But there is one relationship you need to work on strengthening first - *the relationship with yourself.*

Why It Is Important to Understand Yourself Before You Can Analyze Others

If you don't learn how to recognize and identify with yourself, you'll never be able to do that with others, too. At least, not entirely. When you're attempting to learn how to analyze someone else, you're attempting to look for clues which will be indicators about who they are and what they're feeling. However, it is equally important to do the same thing with yourself. When you're looking for clues as to why people react the way that they do, you also need to look for clues about why *you* react the way that you do. Only when you understand yourself entirely, can you then begin to understand others.

To understand and build better connections with the people around you, you need to first understand yourself. If you don't have the necessary self-awareness to begin understanding why you do or say the things that you do, how can you begin to understand someone else's intentions and where they're coming from? Remember, someone else could be reading and assessing your body language, too. Analyzing you the way you may be doing to them. What message do you want them to read?

So, if self-reflection is so important, why don't more people do it? There could be several reasons for that, including:

- **They're Unsure about What Needs to Be Done.** Many people don't necessarily spend enough time in self-reflection because they're simply unsure about what needs to be done. We are quick to analyze others, but when it comes to ourselves, that's where many fall short.

- **They Don't Particularly Enjoy It.** Self-reflection is not always the easiest process, especially because it forces people to confront all the emotions and thoughts that they would prefer to ignore. In fact, it is one of the most difficult skills to master personally. Weaknesses, vulnerability, fears, and more are all the emotions that many people prefer to keep buried or hidden, and self-reflection is a process that is going to force all these unpleasant qualities to the surface, which is why many people don't enjoy this process. For many people, acknowledging the flaws is the most difficult part of the process. Nobody likes to admit they've got faults which they need to work on. Pride and ego get in the way. This is largely responsible for why many people suffer from denial, completely blind to their own faults.

- **They Don't Understand How It Can Help.** As people, we tend to be motivated to do something only if we can see what is in it for us. We need the motivation to get us to do something we may not necessarily like or enjoy. Only if we can clearly see the benefits do we then take action. This is why many people don't spend enough time self-reflecting, because they don't see how this process is going to help them. They don't view it as a good use of their time, especially when they have a busy schedule.

- **They Don't Have Time.** It's a common phrase that is uttered these days. *I don't have time.* There never seems to be enough time to get things done. To those who feel like they are constantly on the move from one task to the next, asking them to spend several minutes in quiet self-reflection doesn't make any sense because they don't see it as a good use of their time.

When you understand yourself and your personality a little better, you'll naturally become more understanding of others, too. If you notice the way that you behave and the body language signals that you emit, you'll be able to understand why someone else might be doing the same thing. If you're an introvert, for instance, you'll be able to acknowledge why other introverts may be displaying certain signals, because you will recognize them in yourself. It works the same way for extroverts, too. Understanding others begins, very simply, with understanding yourself first.

Self-Awareness and Emotional Intelligence

Human emotions remain the driving force of a lot of the things we say, think, and do. Emotions can be a very powerful, volatile force within us that may sometimes have difficulty trying to control. This is why emotional intelligence is linked to self-awareness. A clear sign that someone possesses a high level of emotional intelligence is when they can master and control not just their own emotions, but they can also exercise influence over the emotions of others, too.

Yes, emotional intelligence allows you to influence the way other people are feeling. In fact, you'll be able to understand the people around you even better when you've got emotional intelligence on your side. Made of five core principles, emotional intelligence involves self-awareness, self-reflection, motivation, social skills, and empathy. These five traits are the tools which are going to help you analyze others even better than ever because each of these qualities is working in a way that encourages you to be more observant about a person's body language.

Self-reflection, which is what this chapter has largely been focusing on, is first understanding your own emotions so you can then regulate your responses and reactions (self-regulation). To begin developing a deeper understanding of the people around you is where social skills and empathy come into play. Empathy is the ability to put yourself in someone else's shoes, to see things from their perspective, and to understand where they are coming from and why they feel what they feel. When you can connect with them on this level without them even realizing it, your social skills will then play a role in getting them to open up more and be comfortable around you.

Identifying Your Strengths and Weaknesses

People are quick to talk about strengths, but not everyone likes to admit they have weaknesses. However, the only way you're going to begin developing a great understanding of yourself is by recognizing *both* your strengths and weaknesses together. It isn't going to work if you just acknowledge one, but not the other. Understandably, it's never enjoyable to admit that you have weaknesses. It makes you feel inadequate, and for some people, it feeds into their deep-rooted fear about not being good enough. Others may have a lot of pride, and they simply do not like to admit they have weaknesses because they don't want others to think any less of them.

When you embrace both your strengths and your weaknesses, you begin opening yourself to even greater potential for personal growth. Weaknesses are nothing to be ashamed of. It just means that there are areas for you to work on and you're getting there eventually. This is why self-awareness is so critical.

It puts the power of change in your hands, and you are in control. You are the one who gets to decide if these traits continue to remain weaknesses, or whether you're going to work on them and turn them into strengths.

Everyone should make time to get to know themselves better. The benefits of being more aware of who you are and what makes you tick include:

- **It is the Key to Being Happier.** Chances are if you're not happy, you're mind is going to be too preoccupied to effectively analyze and decipher someone else's body language anyway. The more you understand yourself and your emotions, the happier you will be. It also makes it much easier for you to express your desires.

- **It is the Key to Less Internal Conflict.** Another happiness barrier that many people experience is internal conflict. Understanding yourself allows you to connect to your mind, body, and soul, and when your external actions work in tandem with your internal emotions, the internal struggle that you face becomes significantly less.

- **It is the Key to Tolerance and Understanding.** Analyzing what other people feel is a lot better when you've got tolerance and patience on your side. Your awareness about the emotions and challenges that you face will make you more perceptive towards the plight of others, that they may be going through the same thing you are.

- **It is the Key to More Self-Control.** Knowing yourself also means your values are grounded and you know what your preferences are. It affords you better decision-making abilities because you know what you're willing to put up with, what's acceptable, and what isn't.

- **It is the Key to Succeeding at Work.** Excelling at your job goes beyond just being good at what you do. It involves the way you communicate, the way you relate to others, how well you present yourself and of course, the secret messages that you're revealing through your body language. An employee, for example, may say that they love their job, but their body language could be conveying something completely different. If they aren't self-aware, they won't even realize this is happening. But you know who will notice? The bosses (and your other colleagues who are paying attention).

Effective Tools and Strategies to Help You Analyze Yourself

Most people spend far too much time trying to think about what someone else's body language might be saying and not enough time on what their own body language is saying. Becoming too preoccupied with trying to say all the right words makes it easy to forget that your body could be saying something entirely different. If the person you're in a conversation with is perceptive enough, they'll quickly pick up that your body language and your words are not a match.

Consider this scenario, for example. You've just had a long, hard day at work. You're exhausted, drained, and just looking forward to changing into your pajamas and spending some quiet time alone. Then, the phone rings and your best friend wants to talk to you and she sounds upset over the phone. Because you care deeply about your friend, you meet up with them like they requested and agree to talk it out. However, throughout the conversation, you're constantly stifling your yawns, sitting back with your arms crossed over your chest, and constantly checking your watch every couple of minutes while thinking you're being subtle about it. Your friend picks up on these signals and comes to the conclusion that you're either bored or disinterested and they might become even more upset because of that. They leave, visibly upset while you're wondering if you've said the wrong thing. Obviously, you didn't say the wrong words. In fact, you said everything that your friend wanted to hear. Your body was just telling a much louder different story without you even realizing it.

Analyzing yourself is an exercise which is easier than you might think. Start applying these strategies below to help you master your self-reflection process:

- **Taking Note of Your Feelings Daily:** How often do you find yourself noticing your thoughts? Probably not very often up to this point. That is about to change though because your thoughts are a very important part of who you are. These thoughts drive you more than you realize. It shapes your perceptions, your attitudes, and your responses to the people, situation, and circumstances you find yourself embroiled in. Start spending several minutes a day just pausing to notice and monitor what's on your mind. Are the things that you're thinking positive? Negative? Are you empowering yourself and feeling happy? Or stressed, worried, and imagining a lot of worst case scenarios?

- **Writing It Down:** A thought journal can be your greatest asset in your self-awareness reflective exercise. During these moments when you're stopping to monitor your thought process, think about writing them down. Like a daily log journal of your thought process. Write about everything that you're feeling and don't hold back. Your happiness, sadness, frustration, anger, how you reacted today, and what you thought about doing. Anything and everything goes. Each time you've got a thought, put it down.

- **Evaluating Your Thought Patterns:** Another reason why a thought journal comes in handy is that it gives you a chance to look back and evaluate your thought patterns. At the end of the week when you look back on everything you wrote down, what's a common pattern that occurs? What's a train of thought which tends to repeat itself? We've got so many thoughts running through our minds daily that by the end of the day or week, we've forgotten most of the thoughts we had. With a journal, however, you can go back anytime and evaluate everything that went on, anytime. Even something that happened a few months ago.

- **Noting Your Perceptions:** Did you know that the way you perceive people and situations could sometimes lead you to misread things? Or draw on conclusions and assumptions which may not be entirely accurate. For example, if you were having lunch with a friend and you noticed that their body language or facial expression was signaling that they were in a bad mood. Or perhaps feeling irritated and angry. The way you perceive situations could lead you to believe that perhaps she is angry with you or you did something wrong, even though that may not necessarily be the case. When faced with these types of situations, this is where self-reflection once again proves its importance. By analyzing your beliefs, taking note of what you heard, what you saw and what you felt that led you to perceive a situation in a certain way, you will come to realize that situations are often affected a lot by factors which we may not necessarily be aware of.

- **Knowing Your Values:** Your values provide a crucial insight into who you are as a person at the very core. A lot of your current values are based on the experiences that you've been through. Values change as your life experiences change, and rarely do they stay stagnant throughout a person's life. When you can pinpoint and identify each of your values, it brings you one step closer to connecting with yourself. To deepen your understanding and acceptance that this is who you are as a person, and this is what you value in your life. When you know what you want, achieving your goals becomes much easier.

- **Reflect On Your Past Experiences:** Does the way you behave and react to certain situations now a result of your past experiences? A lot of the signals and subconscious messages that we give off is a reflection of our beliefs, values, and attitudes. Even though we don't realize we're doing it. Which is why, it is important to conduct this self-analysis to get to know yourself on a deeper level.

- **Reflecting On Your Self-Esteem:** This is another challenging aspect for many to confront, especially when they suffer from a lack of confidence. What is the status of your health esteem right now? Do you believe you are confident? Worthy? Worthwhile? Or do you struggle with a crippling belief that people are constantly judging you? That you're never good enough? The levels of your self-esteem will affect your body language and the way that you are perceived by others. If you notice when someone is feeling shy or awkward because they're hunched, nervous-looking, and exhibit nervous mannerisms, you can be sure someone else will notice the same thing about you. No matter how well you believe you may be concealing your true feelings.

- **Be Honest with Yourself:** Be completely honest with yourself, even if you may not like what's reflected back at you. You're not going to be doing yourself any favors if you aren't. It's okay, this is an opportunity for you to work on improvements, and there is nothing to be ashamed of if you realize that you have some less than desirable areas that need to be worked on. Even if you try to pretend those shortcomings don't exist, remember that your body isn't capable of telling a complete lie all the time. Someone, somewhere out there is going to be able to analyze your hidden messages. Learning to understand yourself is how you learn to spot the same signals in someone else when you analyze them.

Other Ways of Getting to Know Yourself

Personality tests can be great because they ask questions that you ordinarily would not consider. There are several types of personality tests available, a lot of which can be found online. Some workplaces even provide personality tests for their staff as part of their training programmes. This can be an interesting way of digging even deeper to find out what you're made of.

While initially, these personality tests could just seem like an interesting way to pass the time, or even a fun activity to do during work training, but they have more merits than they're given credit for. A lot of employers these days have come to realize the importance of these tests, and some even now incorporate personality test type questions as part of their hiring process. Understanding personalities are how employers find the best fit for their company.

Keen to find out your personality type? Here are some worthwhile tests to consider investing in:

- **Myer-Briggs Type Indicator (MBTI).** Still considered one of the most popular personality tests to this day, the MBTI was created by Isabel Myers and Katherine Briggs based on the ideas of Carl Jung, a psychoanalyst.

- **The Winslow Personality Test.** A test which helps to evaluate 24 personality traits to help you find your strengths. This test is best suited for measuring happiness and success in your career.

- **The DISC Personality Test.** DISC here stands for Dominance, Inducement, Submission, and Compliance. This test was developed based on psychologists Walter Clarke and William Marston's ideas. Companies often rely on this test to gauge the suitability of an employee for a position.

- **The HEXACO Personality Model.** Created in 2000, this personality model measures an individual based on honesty-humility, agreeability, emotionality, conscientiousness, extraversion, and how to open a person is to new experiences.

- **The Revised NEO Personality Inventory Test.** This test was initially developed in the 1970s by McCrae and Costa, and in 2005, it was finalized. Dubbed the NEO-PI-R for short, this test aims to measure what is known as the Big-5 personality qualities. The qualities are, in fact, a little similar to HEXACO's personality model where it namely focuses on neuroticism, agreeability, conscientiousness, extraversion, and how to open a person is to new experiences. Each of these five qualities is accompanied by its own subcategory.

Chapter 2: Body Language and Interpretation

There was once a time when films were silent. If you grew up watching those old, black and white Charlie Chaplin movies, you'll notice how actors like him were the pioneers when it came to sending powerful messages via their body language. After all, it was a *silent* movie, how else were they supposed to let the audience know what was going on? But it's through films like that where we realize just how powerful - and important - body language can be. That our bodies can tell a story so powerful we *still* know what's going on despite the absence of words.

When movies started incorporating sound into them, body language emphasis becomes less and less. Eventually, we came to rely on what we hear and notice less of what someone's body is saying when we watch movies. Silent film actors became obscure, along with essential body language reading skills.

Body language was also studied academically by influential individuals like Charles Darwin, who's published 1872 work on *The Expression of Emotions in Man and Animals* made headway for modern studies on people's facial expressions and body language signals. Since then, there have been many of Darwin's ideas which have been validated by others who have conducted similar research. Albert Mehrabian is another researcher who pioneered the study of body language back in the 1950s. What Mehrabian discovered was that the words we use verbally only had a total impact of 7% on messages; while our vocals had a 38% impact. The vocals here include the inflection of our voices, the tone, and other sounds which may come into play. The biggest message impact, however, came from our nonverbal communication, which was a staggering 55%.

Why It Is Important to Know How to Analyze Others

Actions speak louder than words is not just a saying. Humans didn't always have the ability of speech. Back when the early humans still dwelt in caves, they used body language (and grunting) to communicate what they needed. Their bodies and facial expressions were their primary use of communication. They expressed anger, hunger, fear, love, surprise, and more, all without saying a word. All things considered, speech is still relatively a new way in which we relay our messages, compared to body language which has been present for significantly longer. Because it has been around for as long as it has, our bodies say more about us than our words ever will.

The Benefits of Being Able to Read People

The Significance of Body Language in Deciphering Someone's Emotions

Within the first 30-seconds of meeting someone is when you pretty much start to form your first impressions about them. Even if they don't say a word. How? *Body language.* By observing their mannerisms, facial expressions, the way that they carry themselves, these aspects provide little clues into how they behaved and form your perceptions. Whether they realize it or not, the people around you are constantly transmitting messages with their body, and when you know how to analyze them, what to look for, these messages will become more apparent to you than ever. Even complete strangers around you are conveying secret messages with their body. Are they slouching? Are they standing up tall? Are they fidgeting? Are they frowning? Are they smiling? There are a lot of little clues to look out for.

Body language clues are extremely crucial when trying to decipher someone's innermost thoughts and personality. In many ways, it teaches you to become a human lie detector. Lying with your words is easy enough. We can trick our mind to believe or say anything that we want. Lying with our bodies, on the other hand, is something else entirely. No matter how much you try, you can never get your body to execute a lie perfectly enough. There is something that is always going to give away your true intentions.

Being able to analyze someone's body language is a tremendously powerful skill to possess. It puts you in a position of power because you know something that the other person does not. Body language analysis can also prove to be useful in several job aspects, especially when you're trying to resolve a conflict or a crime. Even when conducting job interviews.

Common Types of Body Language Cues

Body language is the most honest language that we have. Research which has been conducted by those studying this area has discovered that the things that we feel tend to show up in the body first, and only seconds later in the conscious mind. Which means by the time these thoughts have reached your mind, it is often too late because your body may have already given you away.

Leaning to analyze and read someone's body language is about trying to understand and learn what a person's true intentions are. Over the years, we may have become good at masking the way that we feel through our words, but not so much throughout the rest of our body. Did you know that the human brain is hardwired to want to try and read someone else's intention? Or even emotions? That's how the mirroring technique works because we're attempting to mirror the way the person is feeling. To empathize and to share in what we think they may be going through. This is part of our evolution, where we have developed this need out of necessity as part of our survival. When we see someone displaying the fear emotion, we instinctively and immediately know how to react to take the action that is needed.

Assessing body language falls into several categories:

- **Dominant Body Language** is when a person wants to be in charge, in control, or in command of either people or the situation. Individuals who have this desire will usually stand tall with their chest puffed out as a way to express dominance.

- **Aggressive Body Language** is apparent when the person demonstrates body language cues which are perceived as threatening.

- **Emotional Body Language** is displayed when an individual is being heavily influenced by their emotions at the moment.

- **Attentive Body Language** is evident when the person is engaged or interested in their surroundings or people.

- **Boredom** is represented in body language which lacks eye contact. Sometimes, this can be followed by repetitive yawning.

- **Defensive Body Language** is demonstrated by those with a desire to protect themselves or withhold information.

- **Closed-Off Body Language** is evident when the person shuts you out through their body language, such as by taking a step or two back away from you or having their arms crossed in front of their chest.

Parts of Your Body That Give Off Signals

Deciphering body language can be complicated. The biggest misconception that we have about body language is that we assume certain gestures have very specific meanings attached to them. When we see a certain gesture, like a person waving their hands, for example, it means that they're definitely saying hello. The truth is body language is ambiguous. Depending on the context, it could have several meanings attached to it. Crossing your arms in front of your chest, for instance, does not necessarily have to mean that you're defensive. It could represent that you're feeling cold, tired, or it could simply mean that you find this position to be the most comfortable for you and that's why you're subconsciously doing it without even giving it a second thought. But to someone who believes that gestures and body language movements mean very specific things, they could misread the situation completely.

The face is a good place to begin if you're attempting to analyze someone via their body language. People like to *think* that they are good at masking and concealing their true feelings, but they're not good enough. Our bodies tend to give us away no matter how hard we try. Our face is where we tend to give off our strongest feelings, even when we try to conceal them. These show up as micro-expressions, which is the sudden "leak" of true emotions which escape the mask we've put on to show the world. Micro-expressions are usually very brief and fleeting, sometimes, lasting for only a split second. But for those who are focused on analyzing body language, a split second is all they need.

Microexpressions are easy to spot when you know what to look for. Let's start with a person's smile, for example. In general, there are five common types of smiles that you could look out for when attempting to analyze someone's body language:

- **A Smile that is Tight-Lipped.** Your first assumption when you see this smile would be that the person is trying to hide their annoyance perhaps. That might be a good guess. But it could hold other meanings to the smile, too. This type of smile - where the lips are stretched tightly across a person's face to the point where it becomes a straight line while still keeping the teeth concealed - could be a signal that the person is attempting to withhold something. Withholding a secret or fighting the urge to speak their mind perhaps because they know it may not be appropriate. This smile can also frequently be spotted on women who are too polite to let someone know they may not be interested. You may also spot this smile among successful, powerful women who may not want to reveal all the secrets to their success. Compare that smile to someone like Richard Branson, for example, who is always spotted with a wide, teeth-baring green and is perfectly happy to divulge helpful information.

- **The Twisted Smile.** It's incredible that we are capable of showing two different emotions on either side of our face. But that is exactly what the twisted smile represents. An example of this smile would be where the side of your brain is responsible for raising your left brows, your left cheek, and the left zygomatic muscles. Now, while the right brain is doing this, the left brain is working to do the opposite. The left side of your brain does all the same things the right side does but pulls it in a downward position instead. These are the movements that result in what is known as "the twisted smile". This smile type often makes an appearance when an individual is being sarcastic during an argument or debate. This smile can often be perceived as obnoxious. While a lot of body language signals can represent several possibilities, depending on the context, this smile most often represents sarcasm. That is because this smile is done more deliberately, and it is a reaction that occurs naturally.

- **The Sideways Smile (Looking Up).** You might recognize this smile as a favorite of the late Princess Diana, who was often photographed with the sideways smile while looking up. The person would have their head turned down and facing away while they simultaneously look up at the same time with a smile that is tight-lipped. It is a signal that the person could be secretive, coy, or playful. Men are taken when women perform this smile because it evokes within them feelings of wanting to protect and care for the women. When

Princess Diana did it, women liked her and men wanted to protect her. This smile often makes an appearance during the courtship stage of a relationship, too. Prince William now uses this smile often to win the hearts and minds of the people.

- **The Drop Jaw (Smile).** This is another smile which, like the twisted smile, is something that is practiced and done consciously. This smile often reflects that the person is being playful or coy. In this instance, a person simply lowers their jaw (like the name implies) to give off the playful impression.

- **The George Bush Grin.** There's a reason while this type of smile was dubbed the George Bush grin, after the former president. That's because he seemed to have a smirk on his face that was almost permanent. The late American anthropologist, Ray Birdwhistell, discovered that smiling amongst the middle-class was found occurring more frequently amongst residents of Nashville, Atlantan, Louisville, and Memphis. But most of all in Texas, where Texans notably smiled more than other American. Texans were so accustomed to smiling that if someone wasn't smiling, someone might assume or wonder if they were angry or upset about something. Contrast this with New Yorkers, for example, who are accustomed to *not* smiling as often that when you spot a smiling person, you might be inclined to ask if something is funny.

Another area you want to pay close attention to is a person's eyes. If someone is avoiding eye contact, there's a strong possibility their uncomfortable, disinterested, nervous, or bored. If their pupils are dilated, it's safe to say that they are comfortable, perhaps, even like you. If they're blinking far too much (in an unnatural way), there's a strong possibility they may not be entirely honest with you. If they look to the left, they could be recalling a genuine memory, and if they look to the right, it could be a sign that they're trying to make something up.

The jaw area is also another good indicator of how a person feels. The next time you're talking to someone, take a quick look at their jaw. Is it clenched? Or relaxed? If you notice their neck muscles may be a little tense, they're giving off signs that they are experiencing a considerable amount of discomfort. They could subconsciously be signaling that they don't want to be a part of this conversation. Or that they may be feeling tense and stressed about something on their minds. Even if what they are telling you with their words may not be conveying that.

Bodily gestures can also be interpreted differently. Here are some of the common body language gestures that you might notice when you start to analyze someone:

- **Having One or Both Arms across Your Body.** This is among the most common, universally used body language gestures. As we've already established, having the arms folded across the chest could mean several different things. This gesture is learned by us, even as young children. If you observed children, they tend to hide behind objects when they perceive someone - or something - as a "threat". As adults, of course, it is deemed unacceptable to run and hide behind an object the way that children do, and therefore, we've turned to fold our arms across our chest. The arms act as a "protective barrier". It is our minds and our bodies unconsciously protecting ourselves from what we believed to be undesirable situations. However, we already know by now that the arms folded gesture could mean several things. It could be a signal that someone is feeling nervous, anxious, defensive, angry, impatient, or perhaps none of the above and they could simply find this position natural and comfortable.

- **Having Both Arms Folded Across Your Chest.** The position of having both arms folded directly across your chest could also hold several meanings. Some people do it because they feel comfortable, while others do it because, on the inside, they feel negatively towards the person or situation. Both arms directly folded across the chest is often perceived to be less than welcoming, and it could put others off because they assume that you're either angry or closed-off to them or your situation. This body language gesture is off-putting to many because it sends the signal that you either do not want to be involved or do not want to participate. It makes those who adopt this stance seem unapproachable. It appears almost as if you were trying to set up a barrier between yourself and the other person.

The way that a person gestures with their hands is another intriguing way of analyzing what emotions or thoughts they may be experiencing. Here are some commonly used hand gestures that depict the following general meanings:

- **Running fingers through the hair** - Uncertain, unsure, or trying to think.

- **Rubbing the brow** - Worried or doubtful.

- **Rubbing the eyes** - Fatigued.

- **Rubbing the ears** - Rubbing behind the ears is an indication the person fears being misunderstood or that they don't understand.

- **Touching the earlobe** - Seeking comfort.

- **Scratching the head** - Deep in thought or confusion (depending on the context).

- **Covering the mouth** - An indication of dishonesty, or that the person does not entirely believe what they are being told. Sometimes, it indicates the person could be thinking about something (depending on the context).
- **Placing index finger on the temple** - Thinking.

- **Touching the Nose** - Associated with lying or feeling pressured.

- **Holding the lips** - An indication of greed.

- **Chin stroking** - Thinking.

- **Outstretched arms** - If this is done with the palms open, it is an indication of the person's openness.

- **Palms facing down** - Confidence, rigidness, or a sense of authority.

How Much Can You Fake It?

Now, humans are capable of choosing the gestures and mannerisms which we want to emit during a speech, for example, or when you're commandeering a meeting. You get to choose the way you project yourself, the hand gestures you want to make, and the stance you want to take while you're speaking. While you're doing all this though, your body is - at the same time - giving out signals which you're not even conscious about. These unconscious emotions are a projection of what you're feeling on the inside.

These gestures may be small and fleeting, but make no mistake that they are still as powerful. The Facial Action Coding System - known as FACS - was developed in 1970 by W.V. Friesen and Paul Ekman. FACS is used to conduct several functions, which include describing, measuring, and interpreting an individual's facial mannerisms and behaviors. FACS was designed to pick up on even the slightest, tiniest facial muscle contractions and movements. It then takes the data and determines which category the facial action that it detected best fits into. What makes FACS so powerful is that it is able to pick up and detect movements and expressions which we may miss with the naked eye. It is a useful device which is often used by those who research human behavior, those working in law enforcement, and even film animators.

There may be times when you may want to conceal how you genuinely feel or even what you may be thinking about. We don't want everyone else to know what's happening on the inside. In that sense, yes, we are able to fake it to a certain extent. But our bodies have a mind of their own. No matter how hard we may try to conceal or consciously control it, your body will still give away tiny little signs and signals that the message you're conveying may not be entirely accurate. To the untrained eye, you may be able to pass off that everything is okay. To those who know what to look out for, they are able to spot signals that everything may not be as it seems.

Chapter 3: Non-verbal Communication

Communication seems like it should be a fairly straightforward process. However, nothing could be further from the truth. It's not just about interpreting and understanding what someone is trying to tell you with their words. It is also about all the other dynamics that are going on, what else the person is saying with their body, whether their verbal message is something that should be taken at face value, or if there is something more which needs to be taken into account. That's the whole point of learning how to analyze people because you're now trying to decipher the hidden meaning. Trying to discover what it is that they are not necessarily telling you right now.

Verbal vs. Non-Verbal

When a person uses language and sound to convey their messages and intentions that is a form of *verbal* communication. Verbal communication is defined as a channel by which people use to express their ideas, concepts, and desires. This form of communication is extremely crucial in several settings including work, home, and everyday life. It is how we teach and how we learn, and we use this form of communication more than any other in our daily survival.

The written word is also associated with the act of verbal communication. When we read the words in front of us, we are mentally repeating them to ourselves in our minds. Sometimes, we may even say it out loud. Verbal communication, therefore, involves *both* sound and the written word. Words are the form of communication by which humans have used to exchange their thoughts and messages, especially when they are not in a face-to-face setting.

One example of verbal communication involves public speaking. This is where communication is conducted and carried out verbally to groups of audiences. Another is interpersonal communication, and this involves a group of people who may be simultaneously listening and talking. Other examples of verbal communication include your everyday conversations with your friends, family members, co-workers, clients, and even random strangers you happen to meet as you go about your day.

Verbal communication matters because it is our primary way of conveying our messages. We rely on this method of communication to:

- Inform, inquire, discuss, argue, and spread information and ideas.

- Teach others and learn from them
- Bond and build relationships
- Achieve our desired outcomes
- Work together as a team or group with others towards achieving a common goal

Nonverbal communication, on the other hand, relies on other forms of communication which do not involve the use of words or sounds. This is the category which body language falls into. When we use gestures, body movements, and facial expressions to convey our intent, which is a form of nonverbal communication. Does nonverbal communication matter as much as verbal communication?

Yes, it does. Perhaps even more.

It cannot be stressed enough just how important it is to make a good first impression. One example of where first impressions are absolutely critical is during a job interview. From the minute you walk into the room and even before you have uttered your first word, you are communicating with your employer in a nonverbal manner. Your posture, facial expression, and even the gestures that you make are going to be the clues that your employer is looking for when they assess you. The same thing goes when you're conducting important business or client meetings. The impression that you leave people with can be a big deciding factor in determining the outcome of your success. Saying all the right words, but with the wrong body language, is not going to get you the desired results that you seek.

What You See vs. What You Hear

From the moment you first meet someone, they leave an impression on you. What kind of impression depends on what they convey with their body language. Learning how to analyze someone is about matching what you currently see and hear in the social setting you find yourself in, and then drawing your own probably conclusions. The human brain tends to only see what we want to see, and you now need to learn to push past those boundaries if you want to truly learn the hidden messages which a person gives away with their subtle body signals and movements.

How well do you think you're able to spot contradicting messages right now? Body language is such a fascinating subject area. It is like unraveling a puzzle as you search for hidden clues and meanings to what you see and hear. Politicians are a good place to start practicing your body analysis skills. Politicians are fascinating because there are some who have been guilty of saying that they believe in something which isn't necessarily true. They often pretend to be someone that they are not. As a result, these individuals spend a lot of their time trying to dodge uncomfortable questions, lying, pretending, and presenting a facade to the public to survive. It is their body language which eventually trips them up and reveals telling clues that all may not necessarily be as it seems.

Types of Nonverbal Communication

Communication is the overall concept. To be effective at it, you must be able to communicate clearly with both your words and your body language. In fact, the two should be in sync with one another, because that is when you send some of your most powerful messages across to the recipient – by combining the power of the spoken word with the equally formidable power of body language.

Some examples of the ways in which we communicate nonverbally include:

- **Facial Expressions** - This is responsible for a large part of what we communicate nonverbally. A smile or a frown can be more powerful than several words strung together. Since the face is often the first part of you that people will notice, even before they hear what you have to say, your facial expressions are your strongest nonverbal contact point.

- **Gesture** - The deliberate signals and movements which we use when we're speaking is also a form of nonverbal communication. Waving, pointing, and using our fingers as numeric indicator amounts are all ways in which we communicate with the absence of words. A perfect example of how powerful gestures can be is in a courtroom, where lawyers are well known for relying on several nonverbal communication methods and techniques in an attempt to sway opinions to win their case.

- **Posture** - Body language also involves the posture that you present. Someone who is feeling confident, for example, stands tall, straight, and proud to silently communicate to the rest of the world that they are feeling confident. Someone who is self-conscious, shy, and awkward, on the other hand, communicates this through hunched shoulders and folded arms across the chest.

- **Proximity** - How closely you're standing to someone (and vice versa) is also a form of nonverbal communication. Proximity could differ depending on cultures, and when someone is not comfortable being too close to you, there will be body language cues which you can look out for. This includes averting eye contact, folding of the arms across the chest, tapping their fingers or feet, and visibly taking a step or two back away from you.

- **Paralinguistic Communication** - Now, these include all the other facets of nonverbal communication aside from body movements and facial expressions. Paralinguistic refers to the inflection of the vocals, the tone, pitch, timbre, and rhythm of your voice. These fall under nonverbal communication - even though it relates back to speech - because it involves the underlying aspects of what a person is saying. The tone of voice that they use, for example, could carry a very different meaning from the words that they utter. When a person says *I'm fine* but in a clipped, short tone that carries an edge of anger in it, that's a significant clue that indicates the person is, in fact, not fine at all.

- **Touch** - Among the most widely used forms of nonverbal communication is the element of touch. Touching is a powerful move or gesture which is capable of conveying a wide range of emotional messages a person may want to communicate with you. A warm embrace, for example, indicates that the person is happy to see you or happy to have you around. Or that they care for you and they're pleased to see you after a long period of time. A quick, brief hug, on the other hand, communicates that the person is probably uncomfortable with the gesture, the situation, or that the person is uncomfortable being around you.

- **Locomotion** - The amount of movement that takes place during a communication process is a clear indicator of how engaged that person is. Let's say that the person you were speaking to is constantly moving about, fidgeting, pacing, or simply gesturing far too much, it inhibits the opportunity for effective communication to take place.

Why Nonverbal Communication Matters

Nonverbal communication is a powerful element, and therefore, it does hold several advantages to its name that make it stand out more against verbal communication. When used together with verbal communication, it can result in effective communication and relationship building sessions. On its own, nonverbal communication is still a mighty force to contend with.

The ability to analyze others based on their nonverbal communication, therefore, is an important skill because:

- It helps you uncover the hidden meaning that the speaker is conveying, so you can then tailor your responses appropriately to suit the situation and cultivate your desired outcome.

- Being able to accurately assess and analyze another person's body language enhances your empathy and social skills (which thus improves your emotional intelligence levels). By learning how to identify the telling facial clues and body movements, you will be able to reach levels of communication that others are not, simply because you can see what others cannot.

- It is a clue to providing valuable information about what the speaker is not saying with their words.

- It is used to express emotions and empathy in a powerful manner.

- It increases your understanding of the messages that you receive. When used in tandem with verbal communication, both these elements combined can provide a deeper, more meaningful insight into the speaker's message.

- Being able to interpret these nonverbal cues effectively is how you gain the upper hand over the other person. It is a well-known fact that misinterpretations can often lead to disastrous effects, so why not try accurately analyzing body language instead?

- It helps to strengthen your relationships. People tend to feel a connection to those who they believe can "understand" them in a way that others can't. Being able to analyze body language gives you this ability because you can see the clues about what's really going on, even when the other person thinks they haven't said a word about it.

- The right gestures and expressions can be a strong substitute when you don't know the right words to say. Hugging your friend or family member with a tight, loving embrace can communicate your love and support more powerfully than words ever will.

- It can be used to reinforce messages when used in the right way. When giving someone directions, for example, pointing the right path to take reinforces their understanding about what you're trying to tell them.

Our non-verbal communication cues are just as important – you might even say of equal importance – to both our verbal and written communication. One cannot exist without the other. To accurately analyze other people, begin by recognizing the importance of *both* these communication forms, not just in others, but in yourself, too. What messages are you transmitting with your body language?

Nonverbal Cues That Convey Confidence at Work

You've got a pretty good idea by now about the nonverbal cues that you need to look for that reveal hidden clues about a person's true desire and intent. But what about the kind of messages *you are communicating with your body language?* What can you do to give out the right nonverbal signals, especially if you want to achieve success in an environment like your place of work? As important as it is to be able to read and analyze others, we need to make sure that we are also giving out the right messages. Just in case someone is analyzing *you* (and you can be sure that there will be at least one or two people who are reading your clues).

Part of what makes successful individuals so, well, *successful* is the fact that they know how to use both verbal and nonverbal communication to their advantage. Specifically nonverbal communication, which they know can send the strongest messages of all. If you notice, successful individuals often stand tall, straight, and with an air of confidence. They smile, they make eye contact, and they move with intent and purpose. They use carefully chosen gestures during speeches, gestures which have been specifically selected to emphasize the impact of their words to project their messages most effectively.

These individuals know how much nonverbal communication matters that they also know how to position themselves in relation to the people around them. They avoid standing too close because they understand that it could be perceived as either threatening or overwhelming. They also avoid standing too far away because they know it might send the wrong message, that they are feeling distant when it may not be the case. They know how to read their surroundings and anticipate what move another person might make. They have made it a point to understand these skills so well that it has enabled them to succeed in their career.

If you want to start excelling in your career, then effective body language is where you start building your foundation. If there was ever a place where nonverbal communication skills matter the most, it is at the workplace. This is where you are observed the most, especially by your managers and superiors. The most successful people who eventually go on to become leaders and managers at the workplace are the ones who are able to make great impressions on everyone they work with because of how well they communicate. You can be the best at your job in every possible way, but if you don't leave the people around you with a positive impression, there's only so far your knowledge and your skills will take you.

Being confident is an important part of becoming an effective communicator overall. As much as you are busy analyzing the body language of the people around you, there is bound to be at least one or two other people who are *analyzing you.* It is not just the body language of others that matter. Your body language matters, too.

When you interact with others around you at the workplace, the moment you show you are confident, you will find it much easier to hold effective conversations with your colleagues and team members that will result in things getting done. Why? Because they are drawn towards your confident approach. Confident people are not thwarted by challenges, they rise to meet them, and this is what people at work want to follow. Somebody who knows what they are doing and is doing it with confidence.

Remember how our nonverbal cues resonate the most powerful messages of all without uttering a word? That's body language for you. Body language is applicable in the workplace, too, perhaps even more so because this is where it really matters. At work, the way you carry yourself and communicate is just as important as how well you get the job done. To convey confidence nonverbally, you need to start by adopting confident body language whenever you step into your workplace. Do not slouch, do not fold or cross your arms, and do not frown or look sullen. Always be positive and project a warm and welcoming manner. Smile and make eye contact with the people you pass by.

Other ways in which you can project confidence with your body include:

- **Power Poses** - Social psychologist, Amy Cuddy, revealed during her TED Talk in 2012 that power poses can be effective when it comes to appearing and feeling more confident. One example of a confident power pose here involves opening your body and positioning it in such a manner that it seems to occupy more "space". Think of the term *larger than life*. Puff your chest out, roll your shoulders back, and avoid hunching like you're trying to hide away from the world.

- **Observing Your Hand Gestures** - All it takes is for the wrong gestures to be used to convey the wrong message entirely. Being observant about your hand gestures is important in order to portray confidence nonverbally at work. You need to be able to achieve this *without* the use of hand gestures which might be misconstrued the wrong way. When explaining an idea, for example, keep your palms open and your fingers together. This is a universal gesture which communicates openness, trust, cooperation, and acceptance.

- **Holding the Eye Contact** – Maintaining eye contact is one of the most basic rules of effective non-verbal communication. When you engage in eye contact with the person you are speaking to, you are, in effect, showing them that you are interested and keen on hearing what they have to say.

- **Being Aware of Your "Space"** – Ideally, you would want to respect an individual's personal space when you're communicating with them. Spacial awareness is as much a part of the nonverbal communication process as your facial expressions and body posture. Pay close attention to the person you are talking to and watch for signs of discomfort, especially if you are in the office. The minute you notice they are not comfortable with your proximity; take a few steps back to create a comfortable enough space between the two of you.

- **Handshakes Can Be More Revealing Than You Think** – You only get one chance to make a powerful first impression, and nothing leaves quite an impact when meeting someone – especially someone new- than the first handshake. Your handshake will be very revealing to the person on the receiving end, and just one limp, a lackluster handshake is all is needed for that person to be turned-off even before the conversation has had a chance to take off. Think of your handshake as your opening line, the introduction that your body is making. Firm, confident handshakes are a must to convey confidence nonverbally.

Chapter 4: Asking the Right Questions

Your ability to effectively analyze someone is going to have a big effect on how well you can deal with them. To understand what they feel and to know what they truly mean are important aspects to think about when you're tailoring or adapting your message to communicate in the best possible way. Aside from reading their body language cues and signals, asking the right questions will provide a revealing insight into a person's mind. The right questions can even trigger different body language signals.

The thing about analyzing people is that everybody is different. No two people are ever going to be the same, not even twins. Everyone will come with their own behavior patterns, quirks, and tendencies. Some people look at the floor when they're speaking, some clear their throat, others like to jiggle their legs when they sit cross-legged, and some like to stroke their neck. All these subtle signs are easy to overlook unless you're paying close attention to them and trying to figure out what they mean.

People display different body language cues for a reason. That reason would depend on their true intentions, which only they will know of since reading minds is the one thing that we cannot do. While we may not be able to read minds, we can certainly read bodily signals and that can be used to our advantage, especially when it's paired with the right, subtly probing questions.

What is Effective Questioning?

If you have spent time around children, you will notice that they ask the most intriguing questions. These questions come from sheer curiosity and a genuine desire to find an answer to what they wonder about. They don't even ask complicated or tricky questions. They simply ask questions which are meant to satisfy their curiosity about what's on their mind. They don't guess. They don't assume. *They simply ask.* At some point along the way, we stop asking these questions and this has caused a lot of complications at times in our interaction with others.

Gathering information is something that humans have been doing for as long as we can remember. You might even say that it has become part of the basic activities or tasks that we do as people. Why this need for collecting information? Because humans have been using this technique to help us solve the problems that we encounter, to learn and discover new information, to help out with our decision-making process, and even to understand the people around us better.

When you get better at asking questions, you get better answers. Answers that will help you better analyze the person in front of you. Effective questions are, in a nutshell, purposeful. Questions are effective when they provoke thoughts. They are effective when they are open-ended without being leading. This means that you ask these questions with a very specific intention in mind. You know what you're looking for and what outcome you want to achieve, and you're now using these questions as a technique towards getting what you want. If you wanted to analyze a friend or someone you know, what better way to do it than through a series of questions which are geared towards encouraging them to reveal themselves and their innermost thoughts.

What Makes a Question Powerful?

Meeting new people is one of the most interesting experiences that we go through. Think about it, every partner, husband, wife, best friend, acquaintance, colleague, and significant other once started off as a stranger. It was through effective conversation, asking the right questions, and reading their body language that helped your relationship develop to the stage that it is in right now. You have probably used questioning techniques more often than you realize as you go about your day, it's just that we haven't given much thought to them until now.

When we encounter someone new, we often do not give much thought to the kind of questions that we tend to ask. But, if you were to start consciously *thinking* about your questioning approach and techniques, the outcome of that encounter can be much better than you realize. Questions are powerful methods of getting to know a person because:

- It can be used to discover vital information that could make a tremendous difference in the outcome of a situation.

- It can be used to forge and strengthen new and existing relationships.

- It can be used to seek clarification for deeper understanding, which then helps to minimize the instances of conflicts happening. Assumptions and jumping to conclusions have a higher tendency of occurring when the right questions aren't used appropriately.

- It can help to diffuse conflict and identify the solution that is needed.

- It establishes a baseline for you to begin analyzing someone. This way, your opinions and impressions are formed on more substance rather than just relying on their body language.

- It helps you spot inconsistencies between what the person may be telling you, and what their facial expressions or body language may be revealing. If they're telling you their okay, but you notice a slight frown between their brows or the downward curve of their mouth, asking the right question can help you gently probe what's really going on and help them feel comfortable enough to reveal themselves to you.

- It enables you to direct a person's thoughts in a particular direction.

- It enables you to assess their responses and provide insight into how they may be feeling about a particular subject.

- It provides better clarity about an issue.

- It provides opportunities for open discussion.

Why it is Important to Develop this Skill (Asking the Right Questions)

The heart of effective communication and being able to bond with others lies in the exchange of information. A lack of understanding can act as a significant relationship barrier. Imagine if you were trying to form a bond with someone and they appeared closed-off, distant, or disinterested. Eventually, you would experience frustration because you're not getting through to them, despite your efforts and there is little chance of a relationship blossoming from that encounter.

Which is why asking the right questions is so crucial. The right questions in the right situation can improve your interactions and encounters in monumental ways. You could have the power to control every interaction you encounter if you know how to relate to the person in front of you. You don't have to know them well nor do you have to be their best friend in order to start doing that. By simply asking the right questions, every stranger or acquaintance you come across can be coaxed into revealing what they think and what they feel.

It is impossible to get to know someone in detail by basing it on their answers alone. That's because people lie (and they often do), especially when they want to hide their true intentions which they know others may find less than desirable. Perhaps, they could even tell you what you want to hear to seem more impressive or to avoid conflict. There could be many reasons why a person could resort to hiding their true intentions. Which is why it is important to develop *both* skills of being able to analyze others and ask the right questions which will help to reveal even more hidden clues into their personality.

The human mind is a natural problem solver, and it is through effective questioning that we resolve the challenges that we come up against. Whether those challenges are work-related, or even attempting to learn how to analyze someone, our minds are working even when we don't realize it, to try and make sense of what's in front of us. Body language has become such a fascinating subject of focus in recent years because of it. Once we started to realize that there is more to us than meets the eye (and the words that come out of our mouth), learning how to analyze body language to find the hidden meanings behind words and gestures are more intriguing than ever.

Effective Questioning Techniques

As you are learning how to decipher a person's behavior, there are several important questions which you should bear in mind. These questions are here to help you develop your critical thinking and to enable you to delve deeper into those hidden meanings which lie behind a subtle gesture or facial expression.

People are giving off clues and signals every day. All we need to do is watch for it and ask the right questions to encourage them to reveal themselves.

These questions can be utilized as often as you'd like until you have gathered the necessary information required. Enough information at least, which will provide you with enough confidence to say *yes, I know what this person is trying to tell me.* The questions you should be asking yourself when attempting to analyze another person include:

- What body language signals or answers have I observed?
- What do these signals or answers mean?
- What are these signals or answers revealing about them?
- How is this significant to what they are telling me now?

There are two types of questioning techniques which you could turn to. These are known as open-ended and closed-ended questions. When attempting to analyze others, what you're aiming for is *open-ended questions.* That's not to say that closed-ended questions don't have their usefulness (because they do), but open-ended questions will get you further in terms of getting to know someone a lot better. This is because closed-ended questions often only serve to elicit short answers which often put an end to a conversation. When the conversation has ended, how are you going to continue with your analysis of the person?

An open-ended question, on the other hand, is more effective for breaking the ice, especially with strangers or acquaintances. These questions are designed to make a person feel comfortable, and if they are comfortable, they're likely to open up a lot more. This relaxed state is when more body language cues and signals arise because the person is not even thinking about it or consciously trying to control it. Open-ended questions can be an extremely beneficial technique in your quest to analyze others, because:

- It provides the opportunity for developing a conversation.
- It provides the opportunity to find out what the person's opinions or feelings are.
- It provides the opportunity to discover greater details which could influence your responses towards them.
- It provides the opportunity for the person to include more information.
- It provides the opportunity for you to learn something that you did not expect.
- It encourages self-expression in the other person, which then leads to more revealing body language cues and signals.

Contrast that with closed-ended questions, on the other hand, which better serve the following purposes:

- To help you conclude a discussion or conversation.
- To help you make a decision.
- When you want a quick answer.
- When you want to compare answers between several people (such as during a survey)

While these two options may be your primary questioning techniques, there are other methods which can be used if you were looking for more specific answers. Here's a look at some other question techniques which can be employed, depending on whether you need them or not:

- **Funnel Questions:** This is useful if you were looking for answers which were to the point and precise, down to the last detail. You'll see a lot of this questioning method used by detectives when they are attempting to take statements from witnesses to help solve a case. Some examples of funnel questions include *how many people were involved? Who was involved? Can you remember the details of the car? What was the color of the shirt that this person was wearing?* The funnel questioning technique is most effective if you start off with closed-ended questions first, and then slowly lead up to more open-ended questions as the person you're talking to starts to get more comfortable.

- **Probing Questions:** Another good questioning technique which helps you to clarify answers to ensure that you understand all the facts right. It is an alternative strategy to uncover more detail, too (as most questions are aimed at doing). This is a good method to fall back on when you're trying to gather information out of someone who may be trying their best to avoid revealing something. Probing questions can sometimes be used to help clarify statements by asking such as *when do you need this by? What new information have you received? What exactly do you mean by this?* Using the *who, what, where, when, and why* method is an effective probing question technique to quickly help you uncover the answers that you need.

- **Leading Questions:** This is a good technique when you're trying to direct the person that you're talking to towards your direction of thinking. These types of questions usually fall along the lines of *how late do you think this task will be? How efficient do you think this method is? Do you think we should go with the first option?* Leading questions should be phrased in such a way that they appear to be personal.

- **Rhetorical Questions:** When you employ this type of questioning technique, you often don't expect them to be accompanied by answers. Rhetorical questions are, in fact, not really questions at all. Instead, they are statements which are phrased in the form of questions. *Didn't John do a marvelous job on the project? Isn't that display absolutely lovely? They have decorated their home wonderfully, haven't they?* These questions are often used to engage the listener and perhaps even draw them towards agreeing with your point of view.

Good Leaders Ask Good Questions

Good leaders know that forging great relationships is one of the cornerstones of success. Without relationships, it would be nearly impossible to succeed because there is only so much you can do on your own. Good leaders know that the path to successful relationships lie in asking the right questions.

The right questions help to build trust, gain understanding, and make the right connections needed to get you one step further. Good leaders are not preoccupied and too focused on having the answers all the time, because *they know* that no one has all the answers all the time. Which is why when they don't know the answer, they turn to *asking the right questions* to get the answers that they see, be it about a situation or a person. Some examples of the right questions to ask include:

- **Easy to Understand Questions** - This one goes without saying. Your questions must be phrased in a manner that is easy for someone else to understand. When preparing your questions, try to put yourself in your receiver's shoes. You may understand what you're trying to accomplish with your questions, but will they? The wrong type of questions, or even questions which are difficult to understand, can quickly shut down a conversation, and that is something that you want to avoid.

- **Specific Questions** - Questions which are too vague or include too much jargon will only make it difficult for others to understand. When they don't understand what you're trying to ask them, they won't be able to provide you with answers which are relevant or accurate. Avoid including too much terminology or unnecessary language in your questions, and instead, focus on keeping them short, succinct, and as precise as possible. Those are the types of questions that good leaders ask.

- **Neutral Questions** - Good leaders steer clear from questions which are either too positive or too negative. Instead, they choose to reframe their questions so that it enables more discussion and exploration. Effective leaders are open-minded and willing to listen to both sides of the argument, and their questions are designed to reflect that neutral stance. This enables them to analyze where all parties involved are coming from, how they feel, and what they think, which then gives these leaders the power to tailor a suitable solution that will keep everyone happy.

- **Questions That Get Right to the Point** - Leaders know how to get right to the point with their questions, and to filter out the information which is unnecessary. Examples of these questions include *why this is happening? How does this affect me or my team? What assumptions are we making in this scenario? What information do we not know yet?*

- **Questions That Inspire Optimism** - Good leaders are advocates for positivity and optimism. They know that negativity can kill dreams and put an end to optimism. What makes them great leaders is that they aspire to inspire optimism and positivity, and one approach to doing this is by asking questions that will inspire imagination, creativity, and rekindle that fire which is capable of driving anyone to success.

- **Questions Which Encourage Teamwork -** Managing a group of people with different personalities and getting them to work together towards a collaborative goal can be a challenge sometimes. Nobody knows this better than leaders do. Which is why, they value the importance of asking the right questions because well-constructed questions can help alleviate the challenges that come with working in a team.

- **Curiosity-Led Questions:** A leader is someone who is always thirsting for knowledge, someone who never stops learning, and someone who is always curious about the world around them. Especially *the people* around them. They let curiosity lead the way when asking questions, and they are not afraid of looking silly or ridiculous. When curiosity is the one leading the charge, it comes from a place of genuine passion to discover answers. This passion, in turn, is what's responsible for asking the right kind of questions that will work to inspire and drive change.

Leadership is about asking questions which can help to do two things - convey who they are as leaders and work to establish credibility. Leaders are not afraid of questions, and they place emphasis on framing their questions well in order to enhance their understanding of what is going on. Oprah Winfrey, Barbara Walters, and Larry King are examples of successful individuals who have mastered the art of asking the right questions which enable them to convey their expertise and what they value.

Good leaders don't just know the right questions to ask, they also know that *listening* is just as important to building relationships and analyzing people. When the person is speaking to you, focus on the word that they are saying instead of concentrating too much on how you're going to respond. If you miss what they're saying, you won't be able to ask the right follow up questions, and this is something that good leaders tend to avoid. Missing out on crucial information leads to misunderstanding, and when you're a leader, you must never be afraid of asking for more clarification if and when it is necessary.

Chapter 5: How to Interpret Personality Types

On a daily basis, we look at people and try to describe them and assess who they are based on our interaction with them. We use words like 'She's so easy to talk to you' or 'He has such a great personality' or 'I love working with her. Her personality is really motivating'. We use the word personality many times to give a positive or negative assessment of a person but many people are not very sure what personality actually is and what the psychology of personality is all about.

Despite not knowing what personality actually is, our assessment of a person, how they behave and why they behave in such a way are similar to the assessments that personality psychologists do as well. Our assessments are usually very informal and they focus more on individuals. Psychologists, on the other hand, use the conceptions of personality which can be applied to everyone.

This study of personality has brought to the development of various theories that explain how and why certain personality traits develop. Here is what psychologists mean when they talk about a person's personality as well as how do they study it and some important theories regarding personality:

Definitions of Personality

There are plenty of personality theories and the most important thing to do is to understand what exactly personality is.

Personality has Latin origins and it is derived from the Latin word *persona* which refers to the theatrical mask that performers usually wear to disguise their identities or play or project different roles.

A succinct definition of personality is that it involves the characteristic patterns of feelings, thoughts, and behaviors, making each person unique. Also, personality comes from inside an individual and it will remain fairly consistent all throughout their lives unless there is a deliberate attempt to change it. Our personalities are unique and it is what makes us, us.

According to Raymond B. Cattell, personality is defined by what permits a prediction of an individual in a certain situation. Walter Mischel, however, describes personality as patterns of behavior that is distinctive and it characterizes each person enduringly. This personality refers not only to behavior but also feelings, emotions as well as actions.

David C. Funder has a more interesting take on personality. He defines personality as a person's characteristic patterns of emotions, thoughts, and behavior and all of this is a psychological mechanism, whether hidden or not. In truth, personality theorists do not confine themselves to just one single definition of what a personality is. However, we can all agree that personality can be described as a pattern that involves an individual's permanent traits in addition to their distinctive characteristics. These traits give consistency and individuality to a person's life of thought and behavior.

As there are many different thoughts on the definition of personality, psychologists usually focus on the patterns of behaviors and characteristics that can help explain and predict the way someone behaves. These explanations can be focused on different influences such as from genetic explanations, the role of the environment as well as the experience that a person goes through in life. All of these shape their behaviors, their traits, and their thoughts.

Another aspect that does play a role in the expression and development of personality is environmental factors such as culture and parenting. How a child is raised can depend on their individual personalities as well as the parenting styles that they go through, and also the societal expectations and norms of different cultures.

Components

What are the components that define or make up a personality? When we look at the definitions above, you'd think that a person's personality is made of components of patterns and traits. While this is correct, it is not entirely what makes a personality. Some other core components of personality are:

- Consistency: There are a recognizable regularity and order to the behaviors seen. People generally act or behave in the same ways no matter what the situation.
- Psychological and physiological: While most agree that personality is a product of psychological form, research also points to personality being influenced by biological needs and processes.
- Behaviors and actions: Personality also has an immense effect on what causes us to act, behave, move, and response in certain ways
- Multiple expressions: When we talk about personality, it extends above and beyond behaviors. Personality is also seen in our feelings, thoughts, social interactions as well as our close relationships.

Psychology Applications

How personality develops and changes over a person's lifetime is an extremely exciting element of life that one can study. This study and the results gained serves as an important tool to understand the practical applications of the real-world, why people act and behave a certain way and what motivates the behaviors and thoughts.

In most cases, to study a person's personality, personality assessment tests are usually done to help people understand and learn more about themselves and their weaknesses, their preferences, and of course, their strengths. These assessments may focus on how people level on certain traits on whether they rank high on conscientiousness, extroversion as well as openness. Some assessments, though, focus on specific aspects of changes in personality over a course of time, whereas certain assessments are used to help people determine the kinds of careers that go well with their existing personality and how they can perform certain job tasks.

Personality- Competing Views

There are plenty of competing views on personality. There are two views that are competing here which are the ideographic view and the nomothetic view.

- Ideographic view- views personality as unique to an individual. No two people can be compared with one another because their psychological components are integrated as an entirety and not as a sequence of comparable characteristics.
- Nomothetic view- is the view that personality traits can be compared among individuals and each person has a scale of that trait. This unique personality is seen by mapping their position along these traits.

The Myers-Briggs Indicator

The Myers-Briggs Type Indicator is, by far, the most popular and commonly used personality tests. It was developed by Katherine Briggs and Isabel Briggs Myers, a mother-daughter psychologists team.

They created a typing system based on the work by Carl Jung who is a prominent psychologist back in the early developments of this field.

This team created four elements or components to measure personality and each component consisting of a continuum between the extremes of a certain trait. The Myers-Briggs Indicator sought out the answers to these questions:

- How extroverted or introverted a person was?
- How do people learn new information?
- Do they use their physical senses for empirical observation or do they go through intuitive information gathering from looking at details and reasoning?
- Do they do this consciously or unconsciously?
- How do people make certain decisions? Do they go through a logical process or do they go by feeling?
- How does a person deal with the things that are happening around them?
- Do these people project their beliefs on a certain situation or do they look into the details and modify or support their beliefs?

Understanding Different Personality Types

What are the different personality types that exist? Personality types are described as psychological classifications that are given to individuals with specific behavioral patterns and tendencies.

Industrial and organizational industrialists use scientific data to study human behavior in several different capacities from the workplace to the home or any other kind of location. Personality tests are then used to designate individuals to certain job roles in the workplace or in organizations or company departments based on the results of these tests.

Personalities can be measured and now that we've established that, let's observe some personality types. As mentioned earlier, the Myers-Briggs Personality Type Indicator is one of the commonly used tests to figure out what each individual's personality is and according to the Myers-Briggs indicator, there are 16 various types of personalities, although, for the purpose of this book, we will discuss the four main personality types.

Four Personality Types

- The Playfuls – Individuals in this group of personality are funny, energetic, enthusiastic, loud, and are generally considered extroverts who love socializing people. On the downside, they are also known to be disorganized, easily distracted, and have a forgiving nature. They've got plenty of ideas, are innovative, creative, and work fast.

- The Peacefuls –This group of people prefer and thrive in order and peace. They are patient, diplomatic, easy going, and prefer to avoid confrontations with people. They are known to be very down to earth people and are quite stable emotionally. They bring balance to companies that are fast-paced and have strengths to build a working team.

- The Powerfuls – They are usually quite authoritative and productive. They are also known to not give up easily and take control of a situation head-on. They are also internally strong, get their points on, and are hard workers whose main aim is to accomplish their goals.

- The Precises- They are exactly as they are described - they value order as well as structure and compliance. They are also organized and are big-time perfectionists. They also put their work before play or social life and only stop working until they are done with their tasks.

When running a company or a business, all kinds of personality types need to be considered. This is to ensure that the company is successful in meeting its goals and objectives since every person is unique and has its own strengths and weaknesses.

Interacting With the Various Personalities

- The Playfuls usually prefer fondness, approval, and attention.
- The Powerfuls are more attracted to credit, loyalty, and appreciation.
- The Precises typically want space to work solo. They prefer quiet and sensitivity.

- The Peacefuls encourage respect, value, and harmony between people in the workplace.

Here are some examples of scenarios between personality types:

- Precises vs. Playfuls

Quite the opposites because Playfuls like the attention around them, whereas, Precises prefer to work by themselves in an environment which is quiet. Playfuls are extroverts, whereas Precises are introverts. A nice way to work with an introverted person is to give them the space they need to work. Small talk is definitely counter-productive to them. According to Dr. Laurie Helgoe's book, *Introvert Power: Why Your Inner Life is Your Hidden Strength,* an introvert enjoys speaking in conversations that are more in depth. They bloom in conversations that stimulate and they find this glorifying.

So, if you have an introverted colleague, one way to connect with them is to avoid small y'all but instead, spark conversations that offer deeper value. Avoid talks about the weather, and instead, get to know them as a person. Ask them about their interests or Hobbies.

In terms of extroverts, they thrive in the presence of people. Playful are more comfortable making eye contact when they speak to a person. They love being part of the team and love it when their work is recognized immensely. Socializing is something extroverts are confident in doing and giving them the social freedom to be creative during work hours helps them in their productivity and in their prioritizing.

Extroversion and introversion are opposites and very different. They work on a continuum rule where when one is high, it usually means that the other use low. When someone feels like they are a mixture of both introversion and extroversion, they are generally known as an ambivert. Ambiverts are individuals that favor both elements of introverts and extroverts equally. They like solitude as much as they like socializing.

Begin by Knowing Your Personality Type

Understanding your personality type helps you understand yourself a little better and also see which kinds of communication styles best fit you. We also learn and understand the personality of our colleagues which means that it helps us work better with them and develop much greater partnerships. This, in turn, creates a friendlier working atmosphere and a cohesive, well-oiled working environment.

The 5 Types of People According to Psychologists

From the friends you choose to the work you do, the passions that you have and even the candidates you vote for, all of these boils down to your personality. People don't really think so much about how their personality affects their course of life. When you understand your personality, you gain better insight into what you are good at and what you are not.

It also helps you gain insight into how the people around you perceive you. Modern day psychologists agree that there are actually five major personality types and this is usually referred to as 'Five Factor Model' and every person possesses some degree of these types in their personality.

1. Conscientiousness

Individuals that score higher in conscientiousness are usually known to be dependable, efficient, well-organized as well as self-sufficient. These individuals prefer to plan their day and their tasks in advance and are always aiming to achieve better. On the other end of the spectrum, individuals who score lower on conscientiousness are usually seen as obsessive and stubborn.

2. Extroversion

Individuals who have a higher score in extroversion thrive in social activity. They are outgoing and can definitely talk and they have no issues being in the spotlight. Sometimes, this can be seen as attention-seeking and domineering.

3. Agreeableness

For people who have higher ranks in the score for agreeableness are known to be kind, trustworthy, and affectionate towards people. They are also known to have pro-social behavior and are committed to altruistic activities and volunteer work. To some people, they may come off as being naive and overly passive.

4. Openness to Experience

Those who score higher in this trait are people who have a broad range of interest as well as vivid imaginations. They are creative and curious and prefer variety over rigidness. People with high openness scores pursue self-actualization through euphoric and intense experiences such as through living abroad, going on self-discovery missions, and meditate retreats. Sometimes, these individuals can also be seen as unpredictable and unfocused.

5. Neuroticism

Those that score high on neuroticism are often regarded as emotionally unstable. They are very likely to be excitable and reactive and they also have higher capacities of having unpleasant emotions such as irritability as well as anxiety. They are also sometimes seen as insecure and unstable.

Understanding the Basics of Personality

The study of personality says that personality remains predominantly stable over time.

For instance, the traits you exhibited as a child may change a little but it usually predicts your behaviors as an adult. People can alter their personality especially if it is destructive to their personal and professional growth and it takes hard work and immense effort to do this. However, this is possible.

Examples of Personality Traits

Before defining who you are through personality indicators and the like, you should first try to understand some examples of personality traits.

These traits can be specified by our attitudes, actions as well as our behaviors. To enable you to discover your own personal traits, you need to ask yourself some questions:

- How do you describe yourself?
- What brought me joy as a child?
- What brings me joy now?
- What is my biggest accomplishment?
- What is my dream?
- What is my fear?

You can write this down in your journal or your laptop or even record the answers to these questions.

Examples of Positive Personality Traits

Most people's personality traits are positive ones and usually, very little of it is negative. These positive traits are:

- Taking responsibility
- Being honest
- Compatibility
- Adaptability
- Drive and determination
- Never giving up
- Compassion and understanding
- Patience

- Courage to do what is right
- Loyalty

Examples of Negative Personality Traits

Life is about balance and where there's good, there is also bad. Whether we want to admit it or not, we also have negative personality traits.

- The probability of lying to avoid responsibility
- Being selfish
- Extremely rigid
- Unyielding to the needs of others
- Extremely lazy and coming up with excuses
- The inability to empathize
- Alienating people
- Becoming angry
- Disloyalty
- Talk bad about others
- Backstabbing

Determining Personality Types

If we go by the Myers-Briggs Indicator, we know that there are at least 16 different personality types. The very fact that there are 16 types goes to show how complex people are and how their emotions and behaviors are all different at varying degrees.

Someone who says something as a joke may actually be sarcastic and while to some, it could not have been a joke at all but the person saying it was serious. A human being cannot fit into one single mold to decide who they are but it is interesting to figure out which of these molds they thrive most in or which reflects them the best.

Your personality type is a result of varying different factors. It can be your upbringing, it can be your environment, it could be traits passed down from your parents, and it could even before your exposure to mass media, and of course, the internet. Whatever it is, a good way to discover which mold you sort of fit into is to look at personality at its scientific core and to take a test. You can also visit a therapist or a psychologist to help you determine which mold is close to defining your personality.

How Do I Create My Personality?

Before we go into the HOW, we need to ask ourselves the question of whether we CAN create our own personality?

The honest answer - you are the only person who can set your own unique personality and no one else can do that. You can be a patient person or an impatient person. You can be extremely responsible or you can be aloof. You can be kind but also be sarcastic at the same time. To find yourself, there is always the need to ask questions especially in relations to different scenarios.

You may or may not be able to change your personality but you can definitely change aspects of your personality by taking active and determined steps towards becoming a more balanced person.

Sometimes, meeting different people, joining an interest group, or even developing or taking up a hobby is one of those ways that you can become a well-rounded individual.

Sports, for example, is great for making a person a better team player, whereas arts and crafts can make a person more patient, and focused and volunteering can help a person to become more empathic and caring.

The little things that you do help you channel more positive traits to your 'self'. When doing so, the negative traits are lessened and are not so prominent.

How Can My Personality Affect Others?

Sometimes, having too much positivity can also be negative. Remember that life is about balance. You cannot expect to be upbeat and happy at the face of tragedy.

You cannot expect people to embrace a new place immediately, especially if they are homesick.

Learning to balance your positive and negative traits is beneficial as it will help you in the situations you have and the people you deal with.

Offering a smile can certainly brighten a person's mood just as how glare can cause a shift of mood.

There are times where we just don't feel like we're up to doing a particular task or if you are having a bad day - when this happens, you can shift this by changing your attitude.

Sulking and complaining will only make you feel more unpleasant and guess what - it'll somehow drag time. Shifting your thoughts and redirecting your mind can help you come out of the mindset you are in and it would help in the tasks that you are doing even if you do not like doing it.

Be All You Can Be

A great way to start your journey towards self-discovery is to understand these different personality traits. One of these ways is to have a journal with you to journal your thoughts, your evocative questions as well as the answers you have on them. It is your choice and preference on how you want to journal this, whether on a private blog or in a book.

Whatever object or way you choose to inscribe these thoughts, you can mold yourself to be the best version possible when you look at the questions you have as well as the answers you give to them. If you are up for the challenge to make positive changes to your personality, then this is a lane that you can go down and explore.

Uncovering your True Self

Finding out our true personality helps us become better individuals with better relationships with the people around us. This isn't to say that you must change yourself and be someone that everyone likes. No. This is about removing or lessening the negative traits that we have in ourselves so that we can relate better to people, perform better at our tasks, and be a person that is happier both inside and out.

If we are stubborn, then altering this personality to become more reasonable or compliant would help you to become a better partner or friend. If you find yourself unfocused and procrastinating often, then changing your mindset and training your mind to focus would help you complete tasks and accomplish your goals at a reasonable timeline.

So, how do you become a better version of yourself? You start by uncovering your true self - who you are, what are your strengths and weaknesses, and which aspect of these traits you want to work on.

- **Realizing your talents**

To unlock what your talents are if you don't know it already or having fully explored it, you can:

- Think about the significant achievements in your life and why you achieved it
- Challenge what you have in life now
- Question why these elements are significant
- List down the lessoned you've learned and how they influence you and what is the type of career you should choose to pursue
- Understanding your personality type

Of course, your personality gets the biggest chunk in understanding self simply because your personality can provide the elements needed to establishing and understanding why you're prone to acting or react in a certain way and help identify which work environment you would best thrive in. To find out your personality type, you can always look for tests such as the Myers Briggs Type Indicator. Doing this can help you understand yourself better and work towards refining your career goals, so it is more aligned to what you like, what you can do, what you are interested in, and where your passions in life.

- **Understand your values and motivations**

Your values and motivations are also indicators of successful career development. We all get motivated based on various different things although money is the most common of all. But what other motivations would you consider as part of the factors for you strive to do better? What are these elements that you could consider to form the foundation of your career a success? Understanding these elements would help you find and stay in a job that gives you career satisfaction over a job well done.

- **Auditing your capabilities and expertise**

Part of understanding one's self is also understanding and exploring what you are good at, where your strengths lie, and what areas you specialize in best. What skills and qualities do you have as a result of your research, hobbies, or even paid or voluntary work experience? If you want to find out, you can use the Vitae Researcher Development Framework (RDF) to map your current capabilities, attributes, and competencies.

- **Understand your learning style**

The path towards career development is paved with plenty of learning opportunities so identifying your most effective and procrastination-free learning capacity can help you pinpoint what kind of training or course you can and should undertake so that you can develop your capabilities and expertise efficiently and effectively. Again, you can use a variety of tools to what style of learning speaks to you best, and one such way is the Learning Style Questionnaire (Honey and Mumford, 1982).

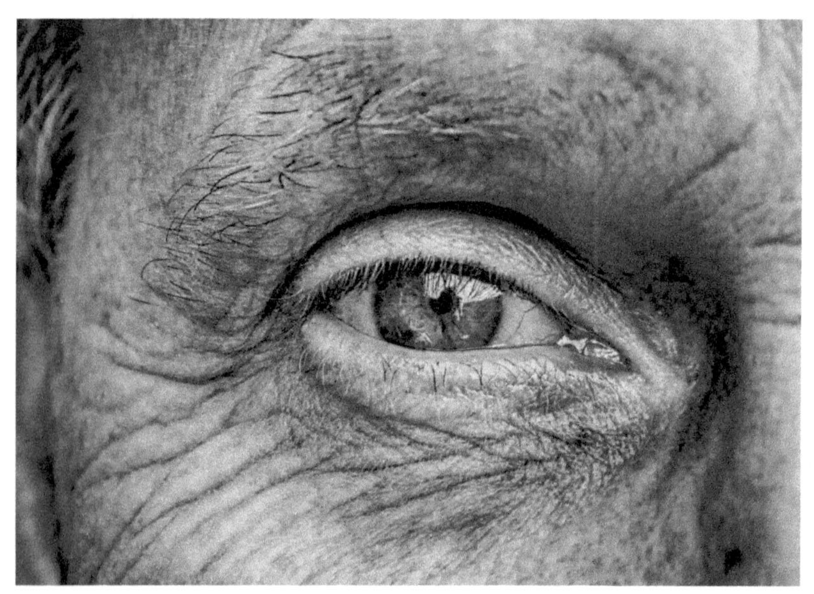

Chapter 6: Behavioral Cues

The Psychological Patterns of Human Behavior

Let's explore analyzing people from a scientific approach and perspective for a moment. For years, researchers - whether academic or commercial - are looking into understanding what governs human behavior; how we decide, remember, or plan for things. In this day and age, wearable technology which is powered by sensors and processes for multi-modal data analysis have enabled researchers around the world to discover and learn about how the human brain works.

Be that as it may, the most challenging part of understanding human behavior is figuring out how our brain supports our natural and ever-changing behavior and cognitive processes. This part is more complex as humans cope with fulfilling evolving physical and mental needs, as well as adapting to our surroundings and environment. The brain is structured in a way that supports all cognitive processes that runs simultaneously with change, and this inevitably translates into our behaviors.

What is Behavior?

According to science, human behavior is built out of a combination of our actions, emotions, and cognition.

An action represents everything that can be externally seen, whether through plain sight or physiological sensors. It is inception or transition from one state to another. To better grasp this, think of a movie being filmed where a director says, "Action!", and the scene is played out. Actions can occur at any time or range and can vary from the simplest form of reactions like sweating and muscle reactions to food consumption, and sleeping patterns.

Cognitions are interpretations of thoughts you capture, and they can come in both verbal and nonverbal signals. Thoughts like, "I have to remember her name," or "I wonder what she thinks of me," are verbal cognitions. On the other hand, picturing how your front porch will look like after a renovation is a form of nonverbal cognition.

Cognitions are also made up of two elements, which are knowledge, and of course, skill. These include understanding how to use a hammer, the ability to cycle without falling off the bicycle, or remembering lyrics to songs.

Generally, emotions consist of conscious experiences characterized by mental activities and feelings that develop as a result of rationalizing or prior knowledge. Emotions range from positive to negative, which determines if they are pleasurable or unpleasurable.

Some parts of physiology such as heart or respiration rate determined by stimulants or arousal tend to not be visible. Emotions, as with cognitions, cannot be seen but can be concluded through facial electromyographic activity, electrocardiogram, facial expression, galvanic skin responses, or respiration sensors.

Actions, cognitions, and emotions are connected in a complex way that enables us to make sense of the world, relate to ourselves, and decide on an appropriate response. Nevertheless, it is not easy to determine the trigger to each response.

Although cognition and emotion are not visible, they definitely determine the output of an action. What we think and feel will drive what action we choose to take. New experiences are combined with our current mindset, which then leads us to adapt to and envision how things may turn out to be according to our actions.

Learning in Behavior

Learning is the acquiring of knowledge, skills, attitudes, social rules, and norms. These new skills or knowledge are formed by both nature and nurture - although there has been an ongoing debate about whether a behavior is formed either through genetic predispositions or the environment. The latest stand, however, is that behavior is considered to be formed by the interaction of both factors.

Classical and Operant Conditioning

A term formed by Ivan Pavlov in 1927, *Classical Conditioning* is a learning method where a stimulus is administered and response follows. For example, saliva is produced when food is served. The food acts as an unconditioned stimulus and salivation is the response. Today, classical conditioning is a widely known basic learning process.

Another type of conditioning is *Operant Conditioning*, which is also known as instrumental conditioning, where behavior is determined by the consequences of an action - in the form of reward or punishment. Behavior is controlled by stimuli which are present when behavior is incentivized or penalized. This method was explored by B.F. Skinner who maintained that it was unnecessary to look into internal desires to interpret or control behavior. Skinner believed that actions which produce desirable outcomes tend to be repeated, and those that lead to punishments are not likely to be repeated. In this sense, positive reinforcement will encourage behavior to be repeated in the future.

These learning theories act as a guide to determine how we gather information about the world. Humans learn through both emotions and physical occurrences, hence, they determine how we behave.

Studying Human Behavior

Aforementioned, tracking human behavior is relatively complex because it is formed and shaped by various factors that the individual may or may not be able to identify. They can vary from voluntary or involuntary, logical or illogical, and overt, or it could be covert.

While some of our actions are guided by what we intentionally and consciously learn and internalize, most of our behaviors are also determined by unconscious processes. Consciousness is the awareness of thoughts and feelings that form perceptions.

Voluntary and Involuntary behavior

Voluntary actions are determined by the individual and driven by the needs-and inclinations of the person. On the contrary, involuntary actions are any executed action without the intention to do so. In terms of the cognitive-behavioral psychotherapy process, patients are exposed to perplexing scenarios such as spiders, social exhibition, or a transatlantic plane ride to help them treat disorders, including phobias, addictions, depression, and anxiety.

Several aspects of the human behavior appear to be voluntary, or rational, or overt, and perhaps even conscious – but they only represent a tiny aspect of what would be deemed normal human behavior. Most of our actions are involuntary, possibly and perhaps even irrational. These actions are controlled by our subconscious. The only way to uncover what this whole other side to our human behavior involves is to attempt to study and analyze covert behaviors which manifest because of our actions.

Rational and irrational behavior

Rational behavior can be considered any action, emotion, or cognition that is influenced or guided by human reason. On the contrary, irrational behavior describes actions that are not objectively logical. People suffering from phobias often report an awareness for their thoughts and fears being irrational, but they are unable to resist the particular urge to behave in a specific way. For instance, a phobia of spiders or holes.

Overt and Covert Behavior

Overt behavior describes any kind of behavior that can be seen, for instance, body movements, physiological processes such as blushing or facial expressions. Pupil dilation might be subtle, but they can still be observed. Covert processes are thoughts (which is cognition), feelings (which is emotion), or responses which are not obviously observed. Subtle changes in bodily processes are hidden from plain sight.

In this case, biometric or physiological sensors are used for quantitative measures as they uncover processes that are covert. Tests like EEG, for example, or the MEG, the fMRI, and the fNIRS monitor a person's physiological processes reflecting the covert behavior.

Measuring Human Behavior

Both academic and commercial researchers have established intricate methods which allow for the collection of data indicative of personality traits. They also enable us to collect data relating to cognitive-affective conditions, along with strategies to help resolve the problems. Generally, these methods of research techniques which are used by these scientists can be categorized into two categories. These are qualitative and quantitative procedures.

Qualitative studies gather non-numerical data and insights. For instance, analyzing diary entries, open questionnaires, or observations produce qualitative data that can be used to understand how those involved in the study perceive the world. It also looked at why they react the way that they do.

Quantitative studies relied on a different approach. They used statistical and either mathematical or computational techniques to produce the numbers that were needed to help them both describe and classify behavior. Examples of quantitative studies include surveys, tests, and observations with coding schemes. In addition, physiological measurements from other sensors produce quantitative output. This then enabled the researchers to transcribe these behavioral observations that they witnessed and turn it into numbers and statistical outputs. We will explore these measurements later in the chapter.

Behavioral Observation

Among the latest tools and methods employed for psychological research on human behavior is *Behavioral Observation*. Researchers could then either choose to study people in their natural surroundings, or they could choose to invite individuals (or groups of individuals) to the laboratory for tests.

Field observations have several benefits. Participants are more likely to be relaxed and less self-conscious when observed from their natural surroundings than at a lab. Most elements are familiar to them, allowing relatively unfiltered observation of behavior, producing a more accurate date.

On the other hand, there's always the risk of uncontrolled distraction. An observation that took place within a laboratory setting, in contrast, allowed for more experimental control. You can remove or exclude any aspects which you did not want, control the room layout to your preference, and ensure that you had set up the best recording environment possible. This enabled researches to create environments which were almost realistic. They could build an office, family room, classroom, living room, and any setting they wanted to put the respondents at ease and make them feel comfortable. Having the respondents in this state allowed for more natural behavior to occur.

Surveys and Questionnaires

Surveys and questionnaires are the quickest ways to capture self-reported behaviors and skills, mental or emotional states, or the personality profiles of your respondents. However, questionnaires are always short momentary snapshots that capture only certain aspects of a person's behavior, thoughts, and emotions. They are highly dependent on how truthful your respondents are to you and how they feel at that point in time.

Focus groups

These groups were usually comprised of a small number of respondents. The range would be anywhere from 5 to 15 people. They would gather with a moderator. From there, these respondents would focus on attitudes and how they felt towards a product or service. Sometimes, this could even extend to an advertisement, ideas, or even perhaps packaging. Focus groups fall into the qualitative tools category. Typical questions revolve around the benefits of a certain product, what are the drawbacks, how can it be better, and who should it be targeted to.

Biometric sensors

In addition to observing conscious behavior, biometric sensors can be used to understand how the mind, brain, and body interact. Biometrics provides insight into hidden processes, and it can also shed light on indications about the thought processes that are largely emotionally driven.

Eye tracking offers accurate insights into visual attention, drawing focus to the various aspects which make up an advertisement. It helps marketers determine how to effectively craft their advertisements or ensure better a user experience. While eye tracking is used on a wide scale to help monitor where we direct our eye movements, there is something else that it does. It tracks the dilation of our pupils.

Electroencephalography (EEG) is a neuroimaging procedure that measures electrical activity generated by the brain using sensors (electrodes) and amplifier systems. It is best for evaluating brain activity associated with perception, cognition, and emotional processes. EEGs, out of all the other biosensors, provide the highest resolution. It is able to surface substantial insights into how our brain's dynamics work, for example, in relation to motivation, engagement, and even frustration.

functional Near-Infrared Spectroscopy (fNIRS), on the other hand, is a system which records the various diffusion of near-infrared light by human skull, scalp, and brain tissue. This process makes it possible for researchers to monitor the human body's cerebral blood flow in very specific regions of the brain. Despite being technology that is still relatively new, it is already proven to be a very, very promising tool indeed when it comes to the research of human behavior.

Electrodermal activity (EDA) is also referred to as the galvanic skin response (GSR). What the EDA does is that it reveals the amount of sweat secretion which is produced from our sweat glands. An increase in the levels of sweat produce results in what is known as higher skin conductivity. When people are exposed to emotional stimulation, they tend to sweat, especially when that stimulation occurs on either the hands or forehead, even the feet. Because the skin's conductance is something which is subconsciously controlled by our minds, it offers vast insight into our unfiltered and unbiased emotional arousal that we are experiencing.

When to use what

While biometric and imaging methods give you exceptional access to an individual's thoughts, feelings, and emotions, the best way to understand someone in entirety is to complement quantitative and qualitative measurements. By combining the measures, we will be able to interpret the process of emotionally driven decisions, as well as slow and deliberate decisions using the insights offered by both routes of investigation.

The Metrics of Human Behavior

Metrics are acquired through methods which include observation, or they could include sensor data. These metrics reflect the cognitive-affective processes which underlie both the overt and covert action that we take. While in general they are extracted through computer-based signals, data can also be extracted through techniques and statistics. Feeling confused? Don't worry; we're going to explore what the most important behavior metrics are for researching people.

Emotional Valence

Perhaps one of the most indicative features when it comes to processing the emotions on your face is emotional valence. Paul Ekman designed the Facial Action Coding System (FACS) which is a very insightful manual into observation techniques. With this system's analysis, data was collected based on the changes detected in muscular activation patterns and facial features. From there, researchers could determine a person's emotional state, which could include anything from confusion, surprise, sadness, contempt, fear, anger, happiness, and more.

Emotional Arousal

While facial expressions can provide great insights into what the general emotional response of a person is, they cannot indicate the level of intensity of the emotion which is being felt. Arousal, in this context, refers to both the physiological and psychological state of when a person is being responsive to a stimulus. This information is relevant for any type of regulation involving human consciousness, attention, and even information processing. The human arousal system is made up of several neural systems in the brainstem and cortex which are interconnected.

Engagement and Motivation (Action Motivation)

This is another human metric behavior which is relevant to the study of cognitive-behavioral motivation. This type of motivation refers to the drive that leads to humans either avoiding or approaching objects and stimuli. Shopping, for example, is a form of behavior which is driven primarily by engagement and our underlying desire (motivation) to want to purchase a product. EEG experiments conductive have given evidence that there are certain brain activity patterns which are detected in certain motivational states. This data can be used to analyze what motivates or drives a person to do what they do, and why they choose to do it.

Psychological Research

Psychologists spend their time to analyze our emotional responses towards our external and internal stimuli. They observe the way that we think, how we view ourselves and the world, how we behave in certain circumstances, and more. Researches measure and modify these stimulus properties during the studies which they conduct to observe and analyze how different personalities and our own individual learning tends to affect the areas of our perceptual, emotional, and cognitive processing.

Conclusion

Human behavior is an intriguing field of study indeed. There is so much to learn in terms of the processes which set the foundation for determining why we act or react the way we do, along with many of our behavior tendencies, despite the fact that we are constantly adapting in response to the environment which we have been put in. Learning how to understand our human behavior pattern is a tricky challenge, which makes learning how to analyze people a challenging process, too. However, we're certainly getting closer towards accomplishing that goal, especially with biometric technology leading the charge.

The Art of Reading People

As explored, there are many stimuli that trigger human responses and lead to decision-making, and researchers have developed extensive methods to measure these outcomes, whether using biometrics, surveys, or focus groups. However, these research methods may not be at your disposal on a daily basis. Below are methods techniques you can use in everyday interactions to analyze cognitive and behavioral processes of individuals around you.

Observe Body Language

Research found that body language accounts for 55% of how we communicate, while words only account for 7%. The tone of voice represents the rest. People can tend to be over-analytical when reading human behavior and it may seem counterintuitive, but in order to be objective in analyzing people, observe naturally and try not to over-analyze.

Appearance

One of the first things that speak the loudest is the appearance of an individual. Take notice of a person's dressing. Is he or she dressed sharply in a suit, traditional clothing, or casual style? Does he or she look particularly conscious about the choice of clothing or hairstyle? The way a person dresses can determine his or her level of self-esteem.

Posture

When reading people's posture, observe if they hold their head high or slouch. Do they walk indecisively or walk with a confident chest? How do they esteem themselves? Posture also reveals confidence levels or a person's physical pain points.

Movements

People generally lean towards things they like, and away from things they do not. Crossed arms and legs suggest self-protection, anger, or defensiveness. When people cross their legs, their toes point to the person they are most comfortable with, or away from those they are not. When hands are placed in pockets, laps, or behind the back, it is an indication that the person is hiding something. Nervousness can also be revealed through lip-biting or cuticle-picking. Some people do that to soothe themselves under pressure or in awkward situations.

Facial Expressions

Aforementioned, emotions may not be visible unless expressed. Frown lines indicate over-thinking or worry, while crow's feet evidence joyfulness. Tension, anger, or bitterness can be seen on pursed lips or clenched jaws. Facial expressions can be one of the most evident ways to read human behavior towards specific things, places, or people.

Sense Emotional Energy

You may have noticed that there are certain people that you enjoy being around more. They lift you up emotionally and improve your mood. On the contrary, being around certain people can be emotionally draining and you naturally move away from these people. These subtle energy signals, though invisible, can be felt mere inches away from the body.

Eyes

Our eyes radiate powerful energies. Almost equivalent to the brain having an electromagnetic signal extending beyond the body, studies indicate that the eyes project this, too. Take time to observe people's eyes and what they transmit: Are they concerned or at ease? Angry or delighted? The eyes can also indicate if the person has room for intimacy or in a defensive mode.

Touch

We share emotional energy through physical contact as well. This can be felt through a handshake, pat on the shoulders, or a hug. Does a handshake feel warm, comfortable, or confident? Or it is brisk and limp, signaling timidity and anxiety.

Tone of Voice and Laugh

The tone and volume of an individual's voice can reveal his or her emotions. Sound frequencies create vibrations. When reading people, notice how their tone of voice makes you feel. Does it intimidate you or make you feel accepted? Is the person avoiding personal questions or shows the intention to continue the conversation? Reading the tone of the voice and volume of laughter can help you better analyze how people feel and predict future behavior.

In the next chapter, we will dive deeper into body language and how they influence relationships. Thoroughly understanding human behavior will allow you to better identify human thought processes and its impact on decision making.

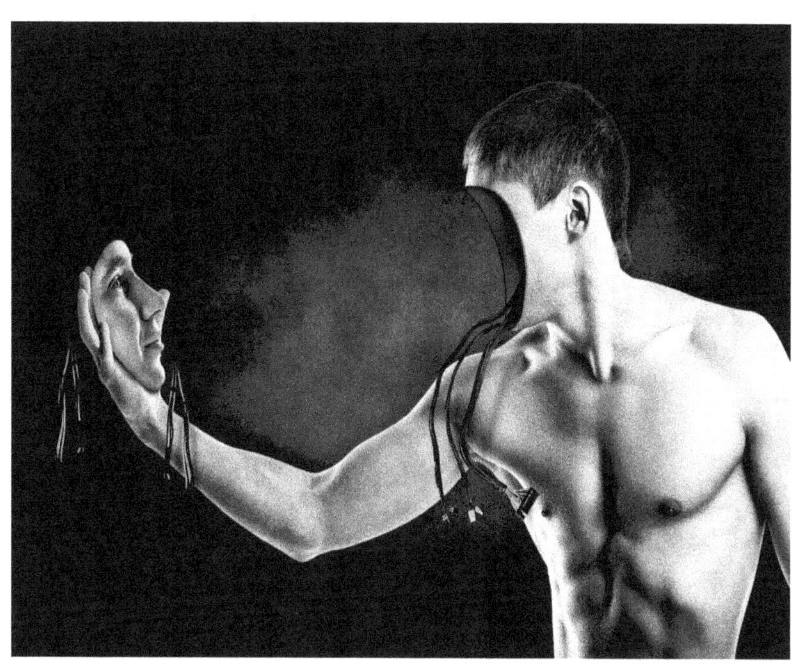

Chapter 7: Affairs of the Heart

If only it were that easy to spot a romantic interest, affairs of the heart would be a whole lot easier. Probably there wouldn't even be a real need for dating websites and apps like Tinder and eHarmony, for example, because we could easily tell when someone was interested. But perhaps, if you knew the signs to look out for, spotting a romantic interest may not be as complicated as you think.

Not everyone can tell with confidence when someone is interested in them. You've probably experienced those moments several times yourself when you think someone may be interested, but you're not *quite* sure and you don't want to risk making a fool of yourself by making the wrong assumptions.

Of course, the game of love is neither simple nor straightforward. It takes a little bit of dating experience to figure out if someone is into you or not or you can just do the good old fashion trial and error. You could get your heart broken (maybe a lot), kiss a lot of toads until you finally, at long last, meet your one true love. Or, you could learn how to analyze people by learning to read the indicators that signal when someone may like you more than just a friend.

Body Language Signals that Indicate Someone is Interested in You

Identifying if someone is interested in you romantically requires the careful and skillful interpretation of signals and actions. The last thing that you want is to read the signals wrong and perhaps end up jeopardizing a perfectly good friendship (if you did start off as friends) because you read the signals wrong and now the situation has just become uncomfortable.

Thankfully, there are certain body language cues and indicators which can help give you a clue as to whether or not someone is, in fact, romantically interested in you. If someone likes you, they mirror your body language and your movements. There are some general body language cues that a person emits if they are romantically interested in someone. For example, they sit or lean in closer, they smile when you smile. They may find ways to touch you, for example, like brushing against your shoulder, putting a strand of your hair behind your ear - all these are classic flirtation signs and if you are uncomfortable, say so, but if you are enjoying it, this person is clearly into you.

Body language has been around since the dawn of time when man existed. Since then, very little has changed when two people want to signal that they have a romantic interest in the opposite sex. Much like how we've got body language cues to tell someone to stay away from us, we've also got cues that signal our interest and that we'd like to pursue it even further. Body language is something that we cannot fool. Once the heart and mind have decided that it likes someone, our body immediately starts to subtly change in several ways that signal our attraction and make it apparent. Those feelings of attraction that a person has are either there, or it isn't, and the body is incapable of telling a lie.

General body language indicators that work on both men and women include the following:

- **Leaning In** - We tend to lean forward when we are engaged or interested in a person. Even if you're not romantically interested in the person, we tend to behave the same way towards friends, family, or people that we like too.

- **Tilting Of The Head** - The next time you're talking to someone you like (or if they're talking to you), take a quick peek at how they position their heads. It is common to feel shy around your love interest, especially when it's still new, but when someone is interested in you, they will try to maintain eye contact and they're head will be tilted slightly to indicate their interest.

- **Blushing -** An oldie, but one that is still effective today. Flushing or blushing is our body's way of mimicking the effects of an orgasm. This is probably one of the most primitive ways in which our bodies can signal that we are interested. That will happen a lot in the early stages of courtship, especially during the initial meeting. It's not a bad thing either! Women, without realizing, like to mimic that same effect through the use of lipstick and blush.

- **Knees and Feet Will Be Pointing In the Direction of the Person -** When we like someone (or when they like us), our bodies - specifically the knees and the feet - subconsciously position in the direction of the person that we're interested in.

- **Mirroring -** Whenever we like a person, we tend to subconsciously mirror their body language, gestures, and movements. All of this without even realizing it. We order the same drink, the same food, and when they smile, we smile. When they move, we move.

How Men Signal Interest

He loves me. He loves me not. It's an age-old question that women have always wondered. Is that handsome stranger I locked eyes with across the room interested in me? Does he find me attractive? Does my boyfriend or partner love me like I think he does? How do I tell if he is attracted to me? A hundred questions are probably running through your mind as you ponder back and forth about whether the man they have their hearts and eyes set on is interested in you as you are in him. A big fear that a lot of women - especially the less confident ones - carry with them is a fear of embarrassing themselves, which can oftentimes lead you to avoid putting yourself out there. History has taught men that they need to be the ones to make the first move. The first kiss, the first date, and even initiate sexual intimacy. That's a lot of pressure on the man's shoulders to make something happen, and women can make it easier by meeting them halfway. If you notice a man doing any of the following, there's a good chance that he's romantically interested in you:

- **He Goes the Extra Mile -** A man will not go out of his way for you if he didn't like you, so if he's going the extra mile, that means he's personally invested in this relationship. Going the extra mile can be anything from helping you run errands, driving all the way across town just to get you your favorite meal, helping you tidy up your apartment, anywhere he can be of help to you, he will. This is his way of showing just how special you are to him because he wouldn't do these things for just anybody.

- **They Prolong Their Conversations With You** - If you observe a man looking for ways to prolong a conversation with you, this is his attempt at showing you he is interested. After all, if you didn't particularly like someone, you would look for ways to cut the conversation short and move on with the rest of your day. Meaningful conversations especially are a way in which men show that they have a deeper interest in you. If they keep asking questions just to keep the conversation going, trying to find out what your likes and dislikes are, showing genuine interest in what you say, this is an old, but a classic sign that they genuinely enjoy your company and want to be around you.

- **You Are His Priority** - He may be busy running around trying to juggle a lot of responsibilities, but a man who is interested in you will still find the time to make you a priority. If he takes the time to rearrange his busy schedule and plans just to meet you for a cup of coffee or to take you out to dinner, he's investing his time and his effort in you.

- **He Talks About the Future** – Usually, it's the women who are thinking about this more often than men do. So if a man has no qualms about talking about his future plans and you're in them, he's definitely interested in you for the long term. Plans for the future can include anything from planning the next few dates to talking about long term plans for the future (marriage, family, kids) if you're in a serious, long-term relationship. The point is, if they're letting you know that you are going to be involved in their future plans, then that's a sign that they are keen on you.

- **He Gets to The Point** - A guy that knows what he wants doesn't beat around the bush. So if he asks you out, it's a definitive indicator that he likes you. Or better yet, if he tells you directly, then you'll know for *sure* that he most definitely likes you romantically. Men are unlikely to play coy or hard to get, when they know what they want, they just go for it.

- **He Finds Reasons to Spend Time With You** - When a man is interested in you, he will find any reason he can to be around you just to spend a little extra time with you. Simple reasons like *I'm just around the area, want to grab a cup of coffee? Are you busy right now? What are you up to? Want to catch a movie? I'm heading that way anyway, let's walk together* are indicators that he enjoys your company and would like to be around you as much as possible. True, these reasons could also just be that the person likes spending time with you simply because you are a cool person to hang out with but if these reasons keep piling up and it only involves just the two of you, it is probably a big sign that this person likes you.

- **He Puts In the Effort to Get to Know You Better -** When a man is romantically interested in you, he will make every effort to get to know you a little better. In fact, he will want to know just about every single thing he can. He wants to know what you like, what you dislike, he wants to know about your family, friends, job, passion, hopes, or dreams, you name it. If you notice that a man is subtly trying to gather information about you in great detail, he could be romantically interested in pursuing this relationship further.

- **He Respects You and Shows You Respect -** A man that likes you will respect you. He shows you respect by never pressuring you into doing anything that you're not ready for, and he treats you with the respect you deserve whenever he's around you. True, he could be doing all this because he is a gentleman by nature, but make no mistake that when he's romantically interested; he's going to go the extra mile with showing you respect, too.

- **He will Make an Effort to See Things From Your Point of View -** When a man is interested, he will do his best to try and be in sync with you as much as possible. He will take your opinions seriously, and try to see things from your perspective instead of flat out disagreeing with you or brushing off your opinions. This is another way of him showing you respect, because he values your opinions, even if you may think they are silly. He will never ridicule or belittle what you think because he wants you to feel comfortable enough to open up to him and share your innermost thoughts.

- **He Wants to Be Part of Your Circle -** A man who likes you as more than just a friend is going to want to be a part of your inner circle. He wants to get to know your family, your friends, and anyone else who matters to you. He wants to form connections and bonds with these people because he knows that they are a huge part of your life, and therefore, he puts in the effort to get to know them because he knows that it will make you happy.

Other body language indicators common among men when they are expressing a romantic interest in someone include:

- Subconsciously raising their eyebrows. Another common variation of this is what is known as the "eyebrow flash", where a man raises and drops his eyebrow in a quick motion.
- His facial expression remains "open".
- His nostrils are slightly flared.
- He parts his lips to indicate his interest. This move is often spotted during the first initial stages of a meeting.
- He grooms himself without realizing it. Examples of this maneuver include stroking their beard (if they have one), smoothing their clothes, or running their hands through their hair in an attempt to groom it.
- He stands tall with his feet slightly apart.
- He stands close to you as much as socially acceptable.
- He will visibly check you out.
- He stands slightly apart in a group as an attempt to get your attention.
- He smiles when you make eye contact.
- He may stand with his hands placed on his hips, which helps to accentuate his physique and size.
- He may play around with the buttons of his jacket if he is wearing one.

- He touches his face when he's looking at you (this is a preening move).
- If he's sitting down, he will subconsciously try to be as close to you as possible by sitting on the edge of his seat.
- He guides you while walking. This is often done by placing his hand on the small of your back.
- He lends you his jacket when you're out together.
- If he has a drink can or beer bottle with him, he can be found fiddling or playing around with the object as a way of expressing his interest.

How Women Signal Interest

There was a time when men were the only ones expected to make the first move if they were interested. They had to woo you, wine and dine you, until finally; romance blossomed into a meaningful relationship. Not today, though. There's nothing wrong with women making the first move too, especially when they suspect that a man might be showing interest. Men are creatures with feelings too, and if you're self-conscious about getting embarrassed, guess what? So are they. No one likes to get their heart broken, squashed, or stomped on, so if you're interested in a man, there's no harm in letting him know.

- **Prolonging Conversations** - Women will look for ways to prolong a conversation too with the man that they are interested in. Just like what men do. This indicator works on both sexes, and if you observe both parties being engaged and interested in keeping the conversational flow going, great news! You are both equally interested in each other.

- **She May be Shy Around You** - Depending on the woman's personality and confidence levels, a woman may be shy when she is interested in you romantically. It's normal for most people to be a little shy around their crush or romantic interest. Both women and men tend to experience this.

- **She Tries to Find Similarities** - Much like how a man tries to be in sync with you by finding common ground, women tend to do the same. They signal their romantic interest by trying to find similarities that you share. If there is a sport, for example, that you're interested in, she will try to find out as much as she can about that activity and try to share in your interest. If there's a particular movie that you like, for example, she may try to watch it too so she can relate to you on that front.

- **Looking Her Best** - When a woman is interested in you, she will go all out to look her best, especially during the initial stages of courtship when you're starting to go out on dates. If she normally puts a lot of effort into her appearance anyway, she'll go one step above that by trying to look even more perfect when she knows the two of you are going to be spending time alone together. Getting her nails and her hair done, finding the perfect outfit, putting a lot of care into her makeup to look extra beautiful tonight are all signals that she is definitely interested in pursuing this relationship as more than just acquaintances or friends.

- **Wearing Perfume** - Not only do women want to look their best, but they also want to smell their best, too. Of course, they may do this on a daily basis, but even more, care goes into how they look when they are particularly interested in someone as more than just friends. She'll definitely spritz on some perfume before a big date, just so you notice that she smells extra good tonight.

- **She Pays Attention** - Even if the subject you're talking about doesn't particularly interest her, she will be hanging onto your every word just because she is interested in you. Men do the same thing by listening and trying to see things from your point of view, as discussed in the points above. Women, too, show this similar characteristic. She notes and remembers all the little details and she gives you her full attention when you talk, and that is how you tell that a woman is interested in you.

- **Intense Eye Contact** - The closer you get to her, the more intense her eye contact will become. The deeper her feelings become for you, the more intense and prolonged her eye contact will be. She'll look lovingly deep into your eyes when she has strong feelings for you, especially when she has fallen in love with you.

Other body language indicators common among women when they are expressing a romantic interest in someone include:

- She will pout her lips (or lick them) while lowering her eyelids and looking upwards.
- She will stand with one hip thrust slightly outwards.
- She may walk with more of a "sway" in her hips than usual.
- She shows off the most vulnerable part of her body, which are her wrists. She may do this without even realizing it.
- She will sit down with her ankles crossed and her knees will be pointing towards the man without her even realizing it.
- She puts her hand under her chin, and this move is known as the "head pedestal" move. She is subconsciously signaling her interest by symbolically

"placing her head in a pedestal" so the man will take notice.

Chapter 8: Caught in A Lie

When your body language and your words don't match, that's when we come off as seemingly deceptive. That's when you get caught in a lie. Anyone who is perceptively watching you could assume that you are being deceptive.

Lying is definitely a relationship killer. When you find it hard to trust someone, it becomes difficult to form a meaningful bond with them. As much as we would love to tell the truth all the time, the reality is a bit more complex than that.

The Psychology of Lying

Lies. They have so much more power than we give them credit for. Lies have been responsible for causing trouble, damaging relationships, destroying trust and reputation. Lying involves two parties - the one who is deceiving, and the one who is being deceived. The deceiver, in this case, purposefully communicates the wrong information and gives false impressions deliberately. Throughout our lives, everyone is going to be playing the role of deceiver at some point, and other times, we could be playing the role of the one who is being deceived.

Why are we so quick to believe someone's lies at times? Are we just plain gullible? Or do we feel so overwhelmed cognitively that it is simply easier to believe what someone is telling us, rather than search for the truth? University of Virginia's psychologist, Bella DePaulo (Ph.D.) conducted a study and found that lying was in fact, a condition of life. DePaulo's study revealed that most people lied at least once or twice in a day. It is as common as brushing your teeth or drinking water. Both men and women did it, and there were some relationships, such as that between a parent and a teenager, in which deception was higher than ever.

We know lying is wrong, yet why do we do it? We use the terms "little white lie" to sometimes even justify our actions and ease our conscience. The simple truth of the matter is, people lie, because they cannot help themselves. It has become almost second nature to us to try and hide the truth when we feel there is a need for it. We use it to bail us out of awkward situations, we use it to strengthen relationships which we know are going to benefit us at some point, we lie to be kind and to spare someone's feelings, we lie to enhance our social standing, and we lie to keep us out of trouble. Lying has become something of a survival mechanism, and that is why humans will always be prone to telling a lie.

Signs Someone Is Lying

Our bodies tend to give us away. There are telltale signs which indicate when someone might be less than honest. Nobody likes being caught in a lie or being told they are a liar. When the lie comes from someone you know, love, or trust, that painful trust can be even more disappointing.

When you get caught lying in a professional setting, that will completely jeopardize your reputation and kill any chance of having a career.

Some scenarios where a person could lie - *or be required to lie -* include the following:

- **When It's Habitual** - A classic scenario of when someone may habitually lie is when they say "I'm fine" even when they are not. Sometimes, this is done out of courtesy because they don't want to burden someone else with their problems. Other times, it could be because they're so used to saying they're fine that it's on autopilot now and they don't even think about it anymore. They may even lie if they don't want to encourage more questions because they don't feel like talking about it or involving someone else in their problems. Everyone has done this at least several times in their life, where they lie about being fine when really they are not.

- **As A Form of Deflection** - Politicians are especially apt at this one, as they rely on extensive use of body language and verbal lies to deflect questions which they don't want to answer. In this scenario, they attempt to deflect you from paying attention to what matters through this form of distraction.

- **When It Is Expected** - In a legal setting is where you would see this happening most often, hence the term *plausible deniability*. This form of lying is expected, perhaps even customary as part of the job. Certain scenarios such as adhering to nondisclosure agreements and cross-company relationships are an expected part of some jobs. Then there are some jobs which require you to think fast on your feet and respond while simultaneously protecting information. In these scenarios, lying is expected of you. Some people also may feel the need to lie because they don't like revealing their weaknesses to others, and they may try to cover that negative trait by lying and turning it into something positive instead.

-

Are They Telling Me The Truth?

How do you spot when someone is potentially telling you a lie? Especially when lying can take on so many forms during the day. The answer? By analyzing them and paying exceptional attention to spot when someone is being dishonest with you. When it comes to analyzing people to potentially spot dishonesty, here's what you need to keep in mind:

- **Observe When They Attempt to Deny:** One of the most important things you need to listen to is the direct denial of an accusation. They will attempt to justify or defend themselves instead of directly addressing the question posed to them. They might respite to giving answers such as *not likely, not exactly, not for the most part* are common examples of what someone might say when they're attempting to deny an accusation. The next time you observe someone not giving you a definitive answer, they might very well be lying for some reason.

- **Avoid Speculating:** Analyzing and speculating are two different things. When someone crosses their arms, we shouldn't just speculate that they are being closed off or annoyed without analyzing all the facts which are presented in front of us. Crossing the arms in front of the chest is a classic example of a body language gesture which often gets misunderstood because it could hold so many meanings to it. What you should do instead is to analyze the other elements which led to this move. Did this person cross their arms in response to a question? The first sign of deceptive behavior that happens in the first five seconds of the question asked will enable you to determine if that question was the one that produced the folded arms. This first clue of deception could even happen while the first question is being asked, which goes to know that this person's brain is moving much faster than the words coming out of the interviewer - it is a sign that they are subconsciously trying to frame their response. Keep an eye out for clusters of behavior, too, and whether this is a direct response to a question.

- **Avoid Being Biased:** Remember the story of the boy who cried wolf? The little boy was dishonest several times until one day, he was finally telling the truth but nobody believed in him anymore. This story goes to show that even dishonest people are capable of telling truths every now and then. To analyze if someone is being dishonest in a situation requires you to focus on the truthful responses they give while filtering out all the other information. There are certain individuals who are capable of telling truths while simultaneously lying at certain points in their story, and by keeping an eye on the essential information, you avoid being distracted by the untruths in their tale.

- **Observing When They're Being Evasive:** Those who tell tall tales often include a lot of unnecessary fluff and long explanations in their stories, all the while never really addressing the issue at hand. Beating around the bush is how you would best sum it up. Redirecting and deflecting their responses is something they have become adept at doing, and they will try to distract you by even sometimes turning your question into another question. *Have I ever done this before? Don't you know me well enough to know that I wouldn't? Don't I have a good reputation?* These are just some of the many examples and ways in which someone might act evasively. If you observe that someone is doing this for a good 15 minutes or more and blatantly avoids directly answering your questions, it could be a good indicator that they are trying not to get caught in a lie.

- **Be On the Lookout for Signs of Aggression:** If someone is quick to anger and becomes defensive when asked a question, that raises a red flag that there may be something going on, more than what they are willing to let on. When an individual begins to get defensive, angry, perhaps even aggressive, they may attempt to turn things around and make it seem like you are the one who is in the wrong. They could accuse you of being biased, discriminatory, and more, making it appear as though it was your fault. The blame game is a common technique used by those who are being dishonest.

- **Observe Their Body Language:** And of course, there is the ever faithful, natural lie detector that never fails - *body language.* A person's words could tell the most convincing, believable story you've ever heard, but their body will give them away before their minds can catch up. A subtle facial gesture is all it takes to give the game away, and if you're keenly observing them, these clues will be hard to miss. A person could touch their face or nose or even cover their mouth or face because this is another subconscious way of hiding a lie. The stress of deception can also cause the skin to turn cold and start itching or even flush - notice when they suddenly scratch their ears or nose. Look out for anchor point movements such as the changes in the arms or even the feet. Has the person suddenly started tapping their feet nervously? Or sweating profusely?

All of these situations are important to watch and you must also watch the cluster of behaviors and activity as opposed to zoning in on only one behavior. Spotting whether someone is telling a lie or the truth can be hard at first. It certainly requires training to efficiently tell if someone is, in fact, lying so don't be disheartened because you're not able to do it right away. It is almost impossible.

When the Face Gives the Game Away

Our faces are one of the most revealing, honest parts of our body. Without saying a word, your face can convey every emotion with such depth that people will be able to tell what you're feeling if it is expressed strongly. Crying, laughing, frowning, stress, anxious, depressed, nervous, all of these emotions flash across our faces when we feel them within us. Sometimes, even though we may want to cover up our feelings, our bodies don't necessarily cooperate and our expressions become apparent on our faces for anyone who is observant to notice.

It is the signals in our body which will reveal the truth at the end of the day. Most of the time, we are completely unaware that our face is giving the game away. We may think we're doing a good job of covering up our emotions and putting on a mask, but without even realizing it, a slight slip of the mask is all it takes for the truth to snake its way out.

The reason why our faces are incapable of hiding the truth is because of the conflicting emotions that are happening within us. Whenever we're occupied with trying to tell a lie, certain thoughts may be going through our minds simultaneously. It is these thoughts that are shown for a split second across our faces. This is what gives us away. This split second emotion is what reveals the way that we truly feel.

Why is it so difficult to tell a lie? Because our subconscious mind knows what's truly going on and it is acting independently from the verbal lie that we are telling everyone else. Which is why our body language becomes out of sync with the words we are saying because our *mind* is not working in sync. Those who rarely tell a lie are the ones who are most easily caught. Since they haven't had much practice, their bodies don't know how to respond fast enough to the contradictory lie that they are telling, which makes their body language signals even more obvious than ever. They may believe that they have been convincing, but their bodies are telling a completely different story through a nervous gesture or a facial twitch which accompanies the lie.

There are certain people who have mastered the art of lying so well that they are much harder to spot. People like lawyers, politicians, actors, TV personalities, and even professional liars, for example, have perfected their technique and refined their body language gestures to a point where their lies become a lot harder to spot. People believe these individuals a lot more easily because the lies are harder to see. How did they accomplish this seemingly miraculous feat of being able to trick the body into not revealing a lie? They spend time practicing. They practice what they think *feels* like the right gestures when they tell a lie, and this long-term practice has been done over a long period of time. They have also practice minimizing their gestures, forcing themselves to keep their bodies calm and neutral when they're lying. It isn't easy, but it is certainly doable through lots and lots of practice.

Spotting a Lie - The Most Common Gestures Used

There are certain gestures which are used more than others during a lie. When you learn how to recognize them, that's when you start recognizing all the other cues to look out for which the lying individual may be displaying. Here are some of the most commonly used gestures during a lie, so the next time you suspect someone may be untruthful to you, see if you can spot the following telltale signs:

- **Covering the Mouth** – Subconsciously, our brain is trying to tell us to stop the lies that are coming out of our mouths. Our bodies know what we're saying isn't true, and the mind is trying to prevent or resist the act of lying, which is why some people inadvertently put their hands across their mouth. An act of trying to "cover up a lie". This gesture can sometimes manifest in the form of someone trying to fit their fist into their mouth, too.

Some people even try to cover up this gesture by pretending to cough. Actors often assume this gesture when they are playing the parts of criminals in movies or TV shows. When the "criminal" gets caught, the actors subtly incorporate this gesture into their acting like their way of cueing the audience in that they are being deceitful and dishonest. If someone uses this gesture when they are speaking, it could be indicative of a lie. If someone exhibits this gesture when *you* are speaking, it could be that they feel *you are hiding something.* We even see this gesture being exhibited in children at times, through the innocuous *"shhhh"* where one finger is placed over the lips to indicate a secret. The next time you notice this gesture in someone, keep an eye out because something may be amiss their story.

- **Nose Touch** - Some people may rub their noses quickly. Some may just rub their nose in one, quick motion which may be almost imperceptible. Whether this indicates someone is fibbing or not would depend on the context. Sometimes, they could be feeling unwell, or their nose could be itchy when certain elements are present. Research conducted by the Smell and Taste Treatment and Research Foundation revealed that when a person lies, a particular chemical which is known as catecholamines gets released. This chemical is then responsible for the swelling of the nose, especially during intentional lying. This is also the chemical that causes someone's blood pressure to increase. When our noses swell thanks to the blood pressure, we're left with a "tingling" sensation which results in an itch in the nose, which explains why some people briskly rub their noses when they're lying. Almost as though they were trying to scratch an itch. Analyzing Bill Clinton's testimony on his affair with Monica Lewinsky, it is noticeable that Clinton rarely ever touched his nose when he was lying. However, when he did lie, there would be a slight frown which lasted only for a split second, followed by a quick nose touch. How do you distinguish between when someone is lying and when they just have an itchy nose? Well, when someone is generally experiencing a nose itch, they will deliberately scratch or rub their nose, whereas those who use the lying gesture involves light strokes to the nose.

- **Eye Rub** - The rubbing of the eyes is our subconscious brain's way of trying to block out what we perceive to be deceitful or distasteful. Men tend to do this more so than women, who will usually exhibit this move in the form of gentle touch motions just below the eye area. Some people exhibit the eye rub maneuver when they want to avoid looking at person directly in the eye because they know they are lying to them.

- **Ear Grab** - Have you ever spotted someone tugging at their earlobe when they answer a question? This gesture is sometimes associated with the act of lying, but at other times, it could be indicative of other things. This gesture is also exhibited by a person who is experiencing anxiety. Again, this move would depend on the context in which it is exhibited. In Italy, for example, the ear grab means something different entirely and is used to signal when someone is effeminate or gay.

- **Neck Scratch** - This often accompanies the ear-grabbing signal. A person who is lying could exhibit this move by scratching the side of their neck just below the earlobe (if they don't do the earlobe move). This gesture is not only used when someone is telling a lie but also gets displayed when they are feeling doubtful or unsure about something. It can be a very telling sign if it is accompanied by verbal cues which contradict this gesture. For instance, if a person says *yes, I can understand where you're coming from* but accompanies it with a neck scratch, this could be an indicator that they do not, in fact, understand at all, and they are just agreeing with you for the sake of doing so.

Conclusion

Thank for making it through to the end of this book. Let's hope it was informative and able to provide you with all of the tools you need to achieve your goals whatever they may be.

You've now put yourself one step ahead when it comes to analyzing people, and when you continuously put all these things you've learned into practice, you'll only improve as your confidence grows.

Learning how to analyze others can be beneficial to you in so many ways. It can help you socially in your daily life, in your career, and in your quest towards success. People surround and revolve around our lives. There is no way around it. We will always need people in our lives to get us one step ahead, and the better you're able to connect with them, the easier it will be for you to understand the people around you.

Finally, if you found this book useful in any way, a review on Amazon is always appreciated!